LANCASHIRE FOOTBALLING GREATS 1946-1991

A collection of 100 biographies of players who have, in their own right, given splendid service to Lancashire football.

Dean Hayes

Didsbury Press

Published by Didsbury Press
Rodcore Ltd
7 Darley Avenue
Didsbury
Manchester
M20 8XE

Tel: 061 434 6495
Fax: 061 445 8155

First published in UK 1991

Typeset, printed and bound by Manchester Free Press
Cover design: Norman Clive, Warrington

ISBN 1 872325 03 3

To my son, Ben, who shares my love of the game.

Acknowledgements
The author wishes to thank the following for their help in producing this book:
The officials of the Lancashire League clubs, the Association of Statisticians, Liverpool Echo and Bolton Central Reference Library.
Thanks to individuals are due to Iain Price, Martin Coane, Denis Henderson, Peter Bell, Graham Morgan, Nick Walker, John Maddocks, Ted Griffith, Roger Harrison and finally Patrick Quinn of Didsbury Press for his encouragement throughout the production of this book.

Didsbury Press gratefully acknowledges the help received in compiling Lancashire Football Greats from the following Photo Libraries, Photo Sales Departments and Photographers:
Suzanne Miles and Rita Rowe at the Manchester Evening News.
Karen Kenny at the Liverpool Daily Post and Echo.
Michael Brown at the Lancashire Evening Telegraph
Howard Talbot of Wally and Howard Talbot Photography (Blackburn).

INTRODUCTION

'Great' is probably the most overworked adjective in the sporting vocabulary. It is inevitable that some people will ask whether there have really been 100 great players representing Lancashire clubs in the last forty-five years. By definition, the great footballers must be outstandingly good at their job and therefore, require a high level of skill. Of course, the truly skilful player lingers in the memory and many of those I've chosen walked straight into the 100. Others had an individual quality or else some outstanding element of their career that demanded inclusion in these pages.

The talent to play football is a timeless quality. All that changes is the fitness level, tactics and techniques; but it is impossible to measure accurately quality and skill. That is why, in the end, it is a matter of personal choice and certainly not everyone will agree that my 100 players all deserve the description great. In making my selections, I have considered my own personal recollections, the statistical side of a player's career and in nearly all cases, I think I have recognised that a great player needs a pretty good supporting cast.

During my research, it became obvious as to why facts and figures are a source of argument and frustration. Even when every effort has been made to get the details correct, they could still be wrong, for in some instances, there are no means of double checking. Often discrepancies do not come to light until a player's career total of appearances and goals scored is added up – this could well be years after the circumstances of disputed goals have been forgotten. However, everything possible has been done to ensure the facts in this book are correct.

Had there been no restriction on numbers, I would have been happy to include players like Harry Johnston, George Farm, Gordon Milne and Trevor Steven. For me, it has been a pleasure to have seen most of these great names in the game play and to those I have not included in my 100, I would say it is their omission that will generate the biggest debate among readers of this book.

Dean Hayes Bolton 1991

100 Lancashire Footballing Greats

Career details: The figures appearing in brackets represent the number of appearances as substitute.

JIMMY ARMFIELD

Birthplace:	Blackpool
Born:	21st September 1935
Position:	Right-Back

Football League Career

	Appearances	Goals
Blackpool	568	6
Total	568	6

England International Appearances	43
Goals	0

In his days at Arnold School, Blackpool, Jimmy Armfield played more rugby than soccer and actually appeared for Lancashire Schoolboys in the handling game. Fortunately for the Seasiders he decided to become a professional footballer after completing his National Service.

His career had started on the right-wing, both at school and in his early days at Blackpool. In an 'A' team game, he had scored two goals when the Blackpool full-back was injured. Armfield took his place and was kept in that position. He signed for Blackpool shortly before his 20th birthday and made his Football League debut on Boxing Day 1954. An injury to Eddie Shimwell subsequently gave Armfield a chance to establish himself in the first team in 1955-56.

Jimmy Armfield is acknowledged as one of the game's first overlapping full-backs. There is no doubt that his early days as a winger gave him a taste for the attacking aspects of his game. He used to push forward and when he saw the opening, he could cross with good effect, the timing of his run being perfect. After playing for the Football League XI and England Under-23s, he made his full debut in unusual circumstances. Just hours after playing for the Under-23s in a 3-0 win in Italy, he and Jimmy Greaves were flown straight out to Rio de Janeiro. His debut in 1959 was in front of 175,000 volatile South Americans. Armfield was at left-back and up against the flying Julinho – England losing 2-0 to the World Cup holders.

Perhaps his best international came against Spain at Wembley in 1960. England won 4-2. Armfield's complete dominance of Real Madrid's flying winger Gento earned him a standing ovation.

Armfield was a very cultured right-back, sharp in the tackle and quick to recover if his winger went past him. Following his display in the World Cup competition in Chile in 1962, this brilliant and stylish player was voted the best right-back in the world. Chilean journalists accorded him that honour, but it has since been generally acknowledged. He captained England on 15 occasions, after taking over from the injured Johnny Haynes at the start of the 1962-63 season. In fact, at one stage, he played in 37 consecutive international matches, ending with a total of 43 appearances.

After 19 years with Blackpool and playing in a club record of 568 League games for the Seasiders, he went into management with Bolton Wanderers. He had tasted the managerial side during the summer of 1969, when he took an F.A. side on a tour of New Zealand and the Far East.

He was appointed manager at Bolton on 19th May 1971. The foundation had been laid in Armfield's first season, for the benefits were reaped in 1972-73 when Bolton secured the Third Division championship. In September 1974, Armfield eventually gave way to an offer from Leeds United and took the Yorkshire side to the 1975 European Cup Final. He left Elland Road in 1978 to become a full-time journalist. Always playing with great enthusiasm, he was a model player both on and off the field.

MANCHESTER EVENING NEWS

JOHN ASTON snr

Birthplace: Manchester
Born: 3rd September 1921
Position: Inside-Forward; Left-Back

Football League Career

	Appearances	Goals
Manchester United	253	29
Total	253	29

England International Appearances	17
Goals	0

As a boy, John Aston played with Ravensbury School and then Clayton Methodist Chapel team, but he never made it to the Manchester Boys XI. He joined Manchester United as an amateur in May 1937 and was apprenticed as an engineer with the English Steel Corporation. He then spent five years in the Marines, playing his wartime football in the inside-forward position.

Demobbed in January 1946, he didn't think he would make the grade in professional football and so looked for a job in engineering. However, United were keen to secure his signature as a professional and so in August of that year, he signed professional forms. He made his League debut the following month in a 1-1 draw with Chelsea at Old Trafford. John Aston was converted from inside-forward to full-back and joined Johnny Carey as one of the most famous full-back pairs of the immediate post-war years. During the pre-match kick-ins, the crowds were given a treat as the two of them punted long passes to each other with deadly accuracy. They had a great understanding, this helping Aston to gain his reputation at left-back, where he won the first of his 17 caps against Denmark in 1948.

Aston was well-built and a robust tackler, using his weight to good advantage. He was a member of United's first 1948 F.A. Cup winning team and of the 1952 Championship winning side.

During the 1950-51 campaign, he was often called upon to help out in the forward line when injuries took their toll and scored 16 goals in his 45 matches, including two in a 3-1 win over Arsenal.

During his international career in which he played at left-back, he partnered many right-backs, including Alf Ramsey. He scored his last goal for Manchester United in April 1954 in a 3-1 win over Sheffield United at Bramall Lane – it was also his last appearance, as illness cut short his career. He had played in 282 matches and scored 30 goals.

He joined the United backroom staff, taking up scouting duties in 1956 and became the chief scout at Old Trafford in August 1970, following the retirement of Joe Armstrong. He was sacked two years later along with manager Frank O'Farrell.

A peaceful, pipe-smoking man, now retired, he helps

part-time in the retail business of his son John, who followed in his father's footsteps at Old Trafford and had a starring role when the European Cup came to Old Trafford in 1968.

MANCHESTER EVENING NEWS

ALAN BALL

Birthplace:	Farnworth
Born:	12th May 1945
Position:	Midfield

Football League Career

	Appearances	Goals
Blackpool	146	46
Everton	208	66
Arsenal	177	45
Southampton	195	11
Bristol Rovers	17	2
Total	743	170

England International Appearances	72
Goals	8

Football mad as a boy, Alan Ball went for trials with Wolves and Bolton but was rejected by both. In the end, it was only the persistence of his footballing father, Alan Ball senior, that persuaded Blackpool to sign him, after Ball junior had gone to Bloomfield Road and offered to play in a trial.

He made his first-team debut for the Seasiders against Liverpool at Anfield in 1962 at 17 years of age. Within twelve months, he had become a regular in the Blackpool side. He was never out of the game, always dashing about all over the pitch to make his presence felt. When Ball first joined Blackpool, Stanley Matthews, then aged 46, had the young midfielder removed from a practice match because instead of passing to Matthews' feet, he was hitting passes he expected Stanley to run on to! Perhaps his only failing, especially in those early days, was his explosive temper, which was usually the result of a burning desire to win. His competitiveness even shone through when he was signing autographs; he would often give himself letters after his name, Alan J Ball WIN. He occasionally overstepped the mark, so great was his enthusiasm. He often found his way into a referee's notebook for arguing or aggressive tackling. He even incurred the wrath of referees as a young boy. When his father scored in a cup-tie at Accrington, he ran onto the pitch in excitement and was carried off by the referee!

Given his England debut in 1965 against Yugoslavia, he went on to star the following year in the World Cup finals. Without doubt his best match was the final itself. His tirelessness, especially during the extra-time, has become legendary and he set up the third and decisive goal for West Ham's Geoff Hurst.

The sight of him running, with socks down round his ankles during the World Cup Final endeared him to the public. Around the time of the World Cup, Bally thought his career and game were standing still and was ambitious for a move. When it became clear he was available, there was a lot of interest, especially from Leeds United and Spurs and even from Italy. But in the end, Everton moved fast and on August 15th 1966, manager Harry Catterick signed him for £110,000.

Alan Ball was just 1.68m tall and weighed only 64kg, but his courage and determination took him into dangerous situations. With the Toffees he went to Wembley in 1968, only to lose to West Bromwich Albion. But in 1970, they won the Championship with Ball continuing to shine for both club and country, being England's best player in the 1970 finals when they tried to defend their title.

Ball had given his World Cup winners' medal to his mother, a decision which prevented its loss when his own home was burgled six years later. Always a firm favourite at Everton, he joined Arsenal in December 1971 for a record £220,000, manager Harry Catterick reasoning that Bally had gone stale trying to rally a flagging Everton side. He later moved to Southampton, where he made over 200 first team appearances in two spells. History proves that the departure of Ball signalled the end of a great Everton team – he was irreplaceable, for English football was no longer producing his blend of ball player.

On his 67th international appearance for his country, the then manager Don Revie made him captain, but five games later he was dropped, because he had broken a curfew.

LIVERPOOL DAILY POST & ECHO

A pocket battleship, Alan Ball always guaranteed his managers a committed performance.

JOHN BARNES

Birthplace: Jamaica
Born: 7th November 1963
Position: Forward

Football League Career

	Appearances	Goals
Watford	232 (1)	65
Liverpool	139	61
Total	371 (1)	126

England International Appearances	63
Goals	11

Jamaican-born John Barnes came to live in England in 1976 when his father was posted to London as Jamaica's military attache. John's attachment to football grew with every day and the following year, when his parents were about to return to Jamaica, he decided to remain in England and devote his life to the game.

He started his footballing life as a defender, but was soon playing up front for Sudbury Court in the Middlesex League. A natural athlete, he represented Middlesex Schools at rugby and hurdling. At Sudbury Court, his skills caught the eye of Watford director and former Arsenal manager, Bertie Mee, who persuaded the 17-year-old to sign professional forms for the Vicarage Road club. He followed three reserve outings by going on as substitute in a Second Division game against Oldham Athletic on 5th September 1981. On 4th May 1982, he helped Watford to beat Wrexham, thus clinching promotion to the First Division. He played for Watford in the 1984 Cup Final defeat by Everton. For six successive seasons, he reached double figures in terms of the number of goals scored – the only player in Watford's history to achieve this feat.

He signed for the Reds in June 1987 for £900,000 – in terms of some of today's inflated transfer fees, the Anfield club had snapped up a bargain. He had played in 286 first-team games for Watford and scored 84 goals.

Of course, he became an instant subject of controversy, since Anfield was not a place where black players flourished. He soon had the Liverpool faithful cheering him, when in only his second match against Oxford, he smashed home a spectacular goal of his own after laying one on for John Aldridge. The Liverpool fans nicknamed him 'Tarmac'- the black Heighway!

A player renowned for his dazzling dribbling and finishing, Barnes can collect passes in full flight and set up many of his own scoring chances with long runs down the wing.

Less than twelve months after making his England debut against Northern Ireland, he confirmed his World Cup potential with a brilliant solo goal against Brazil in Rio de Janeiro. He ran through the entire Brazilian defence and dribbled round the goalkeeper to crack in the opening goal in England's 2-0 win. Even the partisan Brazilian fans applauded the feat.

Although not a great goalscorer, he's a scorer of great goals. He can score with his head or either foot; his speciality being the ability to bend a ball at free-kicks to make spectacular strikes. Of course, his stunning goal against Brazil was unforgettable; in Belgrade, he beat a six-man defensive wall as England beat Yugoslavia. He also struck a brilliant goal against Arsenal in a televised match. His first hat-trick for Liverpool was against Coventry City on 5th May 1990.

His reputation is such that many teams assign two players to mark him when he goes forward. He doesn't enjoy the cold weather and has been known to wear tights and gloves for games in the depths of winter.

A fabulous player, he is regarded as one of the most talented in the world. He was voted Footballer of the Year in his first season at Anfield and won the honour again in 1990, so joining an elite band of players who have managed to win this award twice – it wouldn't surprise me if he collected the award for a third time!

One of the most brilliant entertainers to grace British football since the war, he has given the great Liverpool team an extra dimension.

LIVERPOOL DAILY POST & ECHO

PETER BEARDSLEY

Birthplace:	Newcastle
Born:	18th January 1961
Position:	Forward

Football League Career

	Appearances	Goals
Carlisle United	93 (11)	22
Newcastle United	146 (1)	61
Liverpool	120 (15)	47
Total	359 (27)	130

England International Appearances	49
Goals	8

Peter Beardsley was born in Newcastle in 1961 and learnt to play football by knocking a ball around the back streets with older boys. Playing for Wallsend Boys' Club, he was soon spotted by Carlisle United and immediately signed up. He made his debut for the Brunton Park club in 1979 and became a regular member of the first team, playing in over 100 matches.

He agreed to a move to the Vancouver Whitecaps in 1982, their manager Johnny Giles recognising the player's potential. His football didn't really progress in Canada and he was loaned to Manchester United. After just sixty minutes first-team football at Old Trafford, he was for some unaccountable reason allowed to return to Vancouver.

In 1983, he was signed by Newcastle United for £120,000, the club he had supported and dreamed of playing for as a boy. He formed a formidable partnership with Keegan and Waddle and scored 20 goals in 35 matches, to help the Magpies win promotion to the First Division. Keegan retired and Chris Waddle joined Spurs, but Beardsley stayed to help Newcastle establish themselves in the top flight. The Geordie fans had a new home-grown hero to sing about.

Beardsley's football continued to improve and he made his debut for England on 21st January in the 4-0 win over Egypt, coming on as a substitute. Due to injuries, he was drafted into England's World Cup party of 1986. He didn't start the tournament, but was brought in for the do-or-die match with Poland. He made a telling contribution, setting up Lineker for his goals.

He returned home a star and after one more season with Newcastle, he was signed by Liverpool in July 1987 for a then domestic record fee of £1.9 million. This sum allowed his old club to modernise their ground with a new stand, now known to the Geordie fans as the 'Peter Beardsley' stand.

Dalglish saw Beardsley as his ideal successor – a player of sheer class who seems to delight in his work. Essentially a front striker, he prefers to play a little deeper, running at defences from deep positions. A good dribbler, a deceptive swivel of the hips almost always puts his

LIVERPOOL DAILY POST & ECHO

opponents on the wrong foot. After an awkward settling-in period, he began to thrill the Liverpool fans with his skill, intelligence and tenacity – factors which led to many goals for both Beardsley and his Liverpool colleagues.

Under Dalglish, the combination of Barnes, Aldridge and Beardsley produced probably the most formidable forward line in English football for many years.

Not a great goalscorer, the one he scored in Liverpool's Championship winning 1987-88 season against Arsenal is worth recording. Nutmegging Michael Thomas, he moved forward to chip the ball over the advancing Gunners' 'keeper Lukic to put the match out of the London side's reach.

The latest star to wear the No 7 shirt for Liverpool, he was allowed by Graeme Souness to cross over Stanley Park to Everton, where his vision and trickery are still unlocking the most uncompromising of defences.

COLIN BELL

Birthplace:	Hesleden
Born:	26th February 1946
Position:	Midfield

Football League Career

	Appearances	Goals
Bury	82	25
Manchester City	393 (1)	117
Total	475 (1)	142

England International Appearances	48
Goals	9

Colin Bell began his career with Horden Colliery Welfare, where his potential was spotted by Bury. He made his League debut for the Shakers against Manchester City in February 1964, shortly before his 18th birthday. The following season, he was Bury's leading goalscorer and in March 1966, after scoring 25 goals in 82 games for the Shakers, he signed for City at a fee of £45,000.

He made his debut for City just three days after putting pen to paper, against Derby County on 19th March. It was the season that Manchester City won promotion to the First Division after winning the Second Division Championship. Bell played in the last 11 matches of that campaign, scoring four goals, including one in his debut match.

The following season, with City back in the top flight, he played in all 42 matches and scored 12 goals, including the first of two hat-tricks in a career curtailed by injury. His three goals came in City's 3-1 home win over Stoke. It was his form this season that led him to be selected for a variety of representative matches. He made his England debut in 1968, but it wasn't until after the 1970 World Cup that he began to establish himself in Sir Alf Ramsey's team. His non-stop running and enduring commitment in that infamous World Cup qualifying tie against Poland at Wembley wasn't enough to earn England a place in the finals.

Bell had been signed for City by Joe Mercer, but in 1972 when Mercer left to become general manager at Coventry, Malcolm Allison, who had been coach at Maine Road since 1965, took over. Allison said of Colin Bell: "At first, he didn't seem to grasp his own freakish strength., He was the best, most powerful runner in the business."

For a midfield player whose prodigious running was his prime quality, he was also an outstanding finisher and on 10th September 1974, he hit his second hat-trick for City as they beat Scunthorpe United 6-0 in a League Cup tie. Bell became the midfield mastermind of the thrusting young City side that won the First Division title, F.A. Cup, European Cup-winners' Cup and League Cup in a four year spell in the late 1960s and early 1970s. He played in almost 500 games for City, scoring over 150 goals. He would have scored many more and made more than 48 appearances for England had it not been for a serious knee injury that brought his career to a premature end.

The injury to his knee forced him to miss the whole of the 1976-77 season. There was, though, time for one further honour, a Central League Championship medal in 1977-78, before the injury forced him to retire in August 1979. A model professional, Bell's balance and athleticism earned him the nickname 'Nijinsky' after the racehorse.

MANCHESTER EVENING NEWS

GEORGE BEST

Birthplace:	Belfast
Born:	22nd May 1946
Position:	Winger

Football League Career

	Appearances	Goals
Manchester United	361	137
Stockport County	3	2
Fulham	42	8
Bournemouth	5	0
Total	411	147

Nothern Ireland International Appearances	37
Goals	9

Millions of words have been written about George Best, the unknown from Belfast who became a soccer superstar. He didn't make the Irish schoolboy team because he wasn't strong or big enough, but United's Northern Ireland scout, Bob Bishop, rated him highly and signed him up for Old Trafford. However, the 15-year-old Best was homesick and he and Eric McMordie (later of Middlesborough) caught the night ferry back to Belfast. Upon his return, he settled down under the paternal influence of Matt Busby and even worked afternoons for the Manchester Ship Canal Company just in case football didn't work out! He made his League debut on 14th September 1963, standing in for Ian Moir against West Bromwich Albion. After only 15 League games, Ireland gave him his first cap in the match against Wales at Swansea. Best initially played wide on the left, but soon began to play in a free attacking role, scoring some of the most stunning goals ever seen at Old Trafford.

He won a Championship medal in 1965 and again in 1967, but as things began to go wrong, his frustration began to show as he retaliated against harsh treatment, to earn himself a reputation for indiscipline, while his taste for wine and women began to undermine his consistency on the field.

However, the peak of Best's career came in 1968 when his team won the European Cup at Wembley, beating Benfica 4-1 after extra-time. One of those goals was a superb effort by Best, who rounded goalkeeper Henrique before coolly rolling the ball into an empty net. It was a euphoric night for Manchester United and for Best, the pinnacle of achievement in a season that saw him gain the titles of English and European Footballer of the Year.

George Best had great natural ability – one of the most gifted footballers you could wish to see. He had great speed and awareness, coupled with fantastic dribbling ability. Strong and brave, he was the complete all-round forward.

He was, however, becoming increasingly difficult to manage – missing training and failing to turn up for a match.

Just before 1972, United sacked their manager Frank O'Farrell and issued a statement that George Best would remain on the transfer list and would not be selected for Manchester United again. A letter from George Best announcing his retirement crossed with this. He walked out on United several times and played his last game for them on New Year's Day 1974 in the defeat at Loftus Road. Four days later, he failed to turn up for training yet again and his days at Old Trafford were over.

In November 1975, he joined Stockport County on loan, playing three games for them – his drawing power trebling the County side's home attendance. A spell in the States playing for Los Angeles Aztecs followed before he joined Fulham in September 1976. He later played for Cork in Ireland before returning to America to play for San Diego Sockers, Fort Lauderdale Strikers and San Jose Earthquakes in the N.A.S.L. In 1980-81, he played Scottish League football with Hibernian, returning two seasons later to play for Motherwell. He also turned out for Irish side Glentoran, Bournemouth and several non-League clubs.

After a succession of glamorous girlfriends, a drink problem and several skirmishes with the Law, Best served a prison sentence in 1985.

MANCHESTER EVENING NEWS

George Best was a footballing genius and has gone down in history as one of world football's all-time greats.

ROGER BYRNE

Birthplace:	Manchester
Born:	8th February 1929
Died:	6th February 1958
Position:	Full-Back

Football League Career

	Appearances	Goals
Manchester United	245	17
Total	245	17

England International Appearances	33
Goals	0

Roger Byrne was playing at inside-forward for the Ryder Brow Boys' Club, Gorton, when Bert Whalley saw him, liked what he saw and signed him as an amateur in March 1949. He had to wait until November 1951 before he made his first-team debut in the goalless draw at Anfield. Byrne got his chance at left-back in the place of Bill Redman. He was converted with great success to outside left for the last six games of the season and scored 7 goals. United were unbeaten in that six-match spell and ended the season as First Division champions.

He began the following season on the wing, but after seven games, he reverted to full-back. He was a confident ball-playing back, who was one of the fastest in that position. His speed was quite deceptive – he could recover instantly, although he was seldom beaten. Matt Busby's success at Old Trafford was, in part, always selecting the right man to lead the side. Roger Byrne succeeded Johnny Carey as captain and was no exception to the tradition of great United skippers. He played another part in the overall scheme of things and led the Reds to successive League Championship wins in the mid 1950s and the F.A. Cup in 1957. In fact, when he led the side to Wembley that year, they were going flat out to become the first team this century to achieve the League and Cup double.

Roger Byrne was a player with great tactical foresight that enabled him to dictate the course of play. His experience up front made him one of the great attacking full-backs and he went on to win 33 caps for England in the number three shirt.

He won the first of his caps for England in 1954 when he played against Scotland after appearing for England 'B' and the Football League.

His last League game for the Reds was in the classic encounter at Highbury on 1st February 1958, which United won 5-4.

He perished at Munich with seven of his team-mates, among others. This highly talented full-back had played in 277 games for Manchester United. His remark after the 1957 F.A. Cup Final defeat by Aston Villa was poignant, when he said: "Never mind, we'll be back next year." Manchester United were, but sadly Roger Byrne was not. Eight months after his tragic death, Byrne's wife Joy gave birth to a son – and she named him Roger.

Roger Byrne was a classic player with a great football brain. He was experienced beyond his years – if he'd survived Munich, he would have gone on to become one of England's greatest captains.

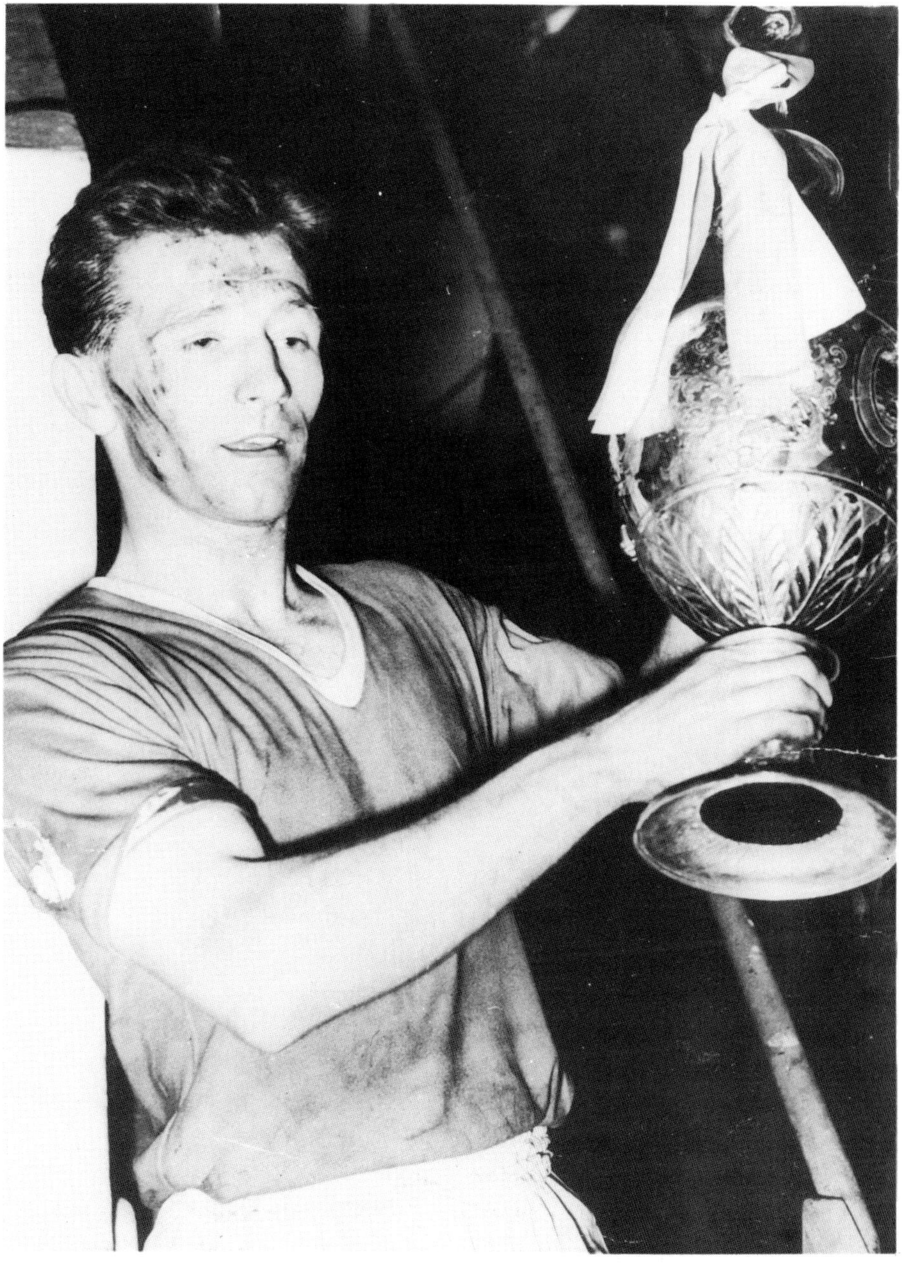

MANCHESTER EVENING NEWS

JOHN BYROM

Birthplace: Blackburn
Born: 8th July 1944
Position: Forward

Football League Career

	Appearances	Goals
Blackburn Rovers	121 (3)	50
Bolton Wanderers	296 (8)	113
Total	417 (11)	163

One of the author's personal favourites, John Byrom joined the Blackburn Rovers' groundstaff straight from school. He had already played for Blackburn Schoolboys and had been capped by England Youth.

After only a handful of games in the Rovers' Central League side, he made his first-team debut against Birmingham City in November 1961. On Boxing Day that season, he hit the first of his four hat-tricks for Blackburn against West Ham at Upton Park. For two years, he jostled for one of the two front places in the Blackburn side, maintaining quite a reasonable goals-per-game ratio. His appearances in the 1963-64 season were restricted to just three games, as the successful McEvoy-Pickering combination proved a handful for opposition defences. When Fred Pickering was sold to Everton, Byrom replaced him and enjoyed his most successful season at Ewood. He scored 25 League goals in his 40 appearances, including hat-tricks against Aston Villa and West Ham (again!).

During the 1965-66 season, Blackburn tumbled towards the Second Division and Byrom struggled to find the net, but in the club's run to the sixth round of the F.A. Cup, he scored 7 goals, including his third hat-trick against West Ham in a 3-3 draw in London.

In June 1966, John Byrom signed for Bolton Wanderers in a £25,000 deal, but the best of 'J.B.' was not seen at Burnden until 1969. The initial idea was for Wyn 'The Leap' Davies to knock the ball down for Byrom to capitalise, but within two months, Davies had joined Newcastle United.

In the 1969-70 season, Byrom started in superb style, scoring hat-tricks in the first two games of the season – Millwall and Rochdale in the League Cup, as the Wanderers won 4-1 and 6-3 respectively. He ended the season with 25 goals from 45 games. The following season saw Bolton relegated to the Third Division and as Bolton's most saleable asset he was put up for sale. Fortunately, for us long-suffering Bolton fans, he stayed to top the Wanderers' goalscoring charts in 1972-73 and win a Third Division championship medal.

On the club's return to the Second Division, he was again top scorer with 24 goals in 40 appearances. In the F.A. Cup tie against Stoke City, he hit a hat-trick in Bolton's 3-2 win, popping up on his own goal-line in the last minute to clear and salute as if he'd just scored the winning goal in an F.A. Cup Final! He 'retired' at the end of the 1975-76 season, after playing in over 350 games for Bolton and scoring 130 goals.

Joining Blackburn for a second time in September 1976 on a free transfer, he found age and a series of injuries were against him and at the end of the season, he finally ended his career.

WALLY & HOWARD TALBOT PHOTOGRAPHY

IAN CALLAGHAN

Birthplace:	Liverpool
Born:	10th April 1942
Position:	Midfield

Football League Career

	Appearances	Goals
Liverpool	637 (3)	50
Swansea	76	1
Crewe Alexandra	15	0
Total	728 (3)	51

England International Appearances	4
Goals	0

Joining the Anfield club on leaving school, he made his League debut in a 4-0 win against Bristol Rovers in April 1960 as a teenager with only 4 Central League games behind him. That first match revealed his ability to judge when to release the ball and when to hold it. Yet, despite the promising start, it was another season and a half before he was given a regular spot in the Liverpool side, as they won promotion to the First Division.

In the top flight, his game blossomed. He was fast and direct, getting to the byline to feed Hunt and St John with the type of crosses that brought the strikers plenty of goals.

Not a great scorer himself, two of his efforts are worth mentioning. Against Everton in 1963, his spectacular 30-yarder sunk the Blues as Liverpool headed for their first championship. Against Inter-Milan in the 1965 European Cup semi-final at Anfield, he sidefooted home from an acute angle after Stevenson and Hunt had worked a well rehearsed free-kick routine.

Though on the small side and slightly built, he was a courageous and determined player. An old fashioned winger, Liverpool turned him into a central midfield player – his appetite for the ball and work-rate being a great influence in the formative years under Bill Shankly.

He only played four times for England, scant reward for such an outstanding club career. He played twice under Alf Ramsey in 1966, but it was eleven years later before he added to the two caps. Manager Ron Greenwood decided to try a block of seven Liverpool players in a friendly against Switzerland. He was 35 when he played his last international game – the fact that he was considered at that age speaks volumes for his fitness and durability.

Ian Callaghan was not a player to grab the headlines, but a player who always gave a fully committed performance for the 90 minutes. He created a tremendous standard of dedication, loyalty and skill, embodying the qualities which built Liverpool into probably the greatest club side in the world.

He won five League Championship medals, one Second Division Championship medal, two F.A. Cup winners' medals, two U.E.F.A. Cup winners' medals and a European

Cup winners' medal. In 1974, he was voted Footballer of the Year. Liverpool's longest-serving player, his last game for the Reds was on 29th March 1978 – a European Cup semi-final first leg against Borussia Moenchengladbach.

On leaving Liverpool, he went to Swansea, helping his old team-mate John Toshack lift the Swans out of the Third Division.

Never cautioned by a referee, Ian Callaghan was deserving of the M.B.E. awarded to him for his services for football.

LIVERPOOL DAILY POST & ECHO

JOHNNY CAREY

Birthplace:	Westland, Nr Dublin
Born:	23rd February 1919
Position:	Full-Back

Football League Career

	Appearances	Goals
Manchester United	304	16
Total	304	16

Northern Ireland International Appearances	7
Goals	0
Republic of Ireland International Appearances	29
Goals	3

Johnny Carey arrived at Old Trafford in 1936 after being spotted by United's chief scout at the time, Louis Rocca. He'd actually gone to Dublin to watch another player, instead he came back with a recommendation that Carey be signed. Rocca later declared that, "No greater Irish player crossed the Channel to make a name in English football."

He made his first-team debut as an inside-forward against Southampton early in the 1937-38 season. He helped United finish Second Division runners-up that season and then played in 32 First Division matches the following campaign.

The war intervened and Carey, though he could have gone back home to Eire, joined up to serve in the Queen's Royal Hussars. When he linked up with Manchester United after the war, Matt Busby was well off for forwards and converted Carey to full-back and made him captain.

Johnny Carey turned out against England in two full international matches within three days and for different countries. He played for Northern Ireland in Belfast on 28th September 1946 and for the Republic of Ireland in Dublin on 30th September. Later in that same season, he played in four countries in eight days. He played at Anfield for Manchester United on Saturday 3rd May 1947 and then for the Republic of Ireland v Portugal at Dublin the next day. He then played in a Dutch trial match at the Hague on 6th May and for the Rest of Europe against Great Britain at Hampden Park on 10th May.

Carey was a man so versatile that he figured in nine different positions for the Reds, ten if you include the occasion he pulled on the goalkeeper's jersey when Jack Crompton was taken ill at an away match. He was also versatile on the international stage, appearing in seven different positions for his country.

He led United to victory in the 1948 F.A. Cup Final over Blackpool and was voted Footballer of the Year in 1949. The following year, he was voted Sportsman of the Year and in 1951-52 led the Reds to the League title, when he was switched to right-half. He played for one more season and then retired.

When that moment came, the United directors took the

unusual step of inviting him to their boardroom to express their appreciation of his long and loyal service to the club. United were keen to keep him on the staff. It was quite obvious that the qualities which made him a great player would be an influence in management and so the directors offered him a position as coach.

However, Blackburn Rovers made him a better offer as coach with more prospects of becoming manager. Things went well at Ewood, Carey taking them into the First Division. This attracted the attention of Everton and after three years in charge, he was cruelly dismissed one Christmas Eve. He took over at Leyton Orient and brought them out of the Second Division, though they went down again after one season. He managed Notts Forest from 1963 to 1968 before returning to Blackburn Rovers as administrative manager; but as Rovers went into the Third Division for the first time in the club's history, it proved to be the end of his management career.

One of the most highly respected men in the game – a superb footballer and inspiring captain – undoubtedly one of the all-time Greats!

MANCHESTER EVENING NEWS

BOBBY CHARLTON

Birthplace:	Ashington
Born:	11th October 1937
Position:	Forward

Football League Career

	Appearances	Goals
Manchester United	604 (2)	199
Preston North End	38	8
Total	642 (2)	207

England International Appearances	106
Goals	49

Born in the football hotbed of the North East of England and the nephew of the legendary centre-forward Jackie Milburn, it soon became clear that young Bobby wasn't just an ordinary footballer. As soon as Joe Armstrong, the United scout, saw him, he knew he had to sign him. He joined United's groundstaff from Hirst North School, Ashington, in June 1953 and turned professional in October 1954. He was a member of the sides which won the F.A. Youth Cup in 1954-55 and 1955-56.

Bobby Charlton made his debut for Manchester United on 6th October 1956 and though he scored twice in United's 4-2 victory over Charlton Athletic, manager Matt Busby felt that the young striker needed time to mature. He explained: "At the moment, Bobby thinks that the game begins and ends 30 yards from the opposing goal. Once he realises he has the whole pitch to play in, he'll be great, just great." It wasn't too long before Bobby learned Busby's lessons well and won a regular place in the United line-up – he was emerging as the youngest of Matt Busby's 'Babes', the young side that was taking English football by storm.

On 5th February 1958, after a European Cup tie in Belgrade, the United's plane crashed in thick snow at Munich Airport. Bobby Charlton was thrown 50 yards and escaped with just a deep cut on his head. He returned to his native north-east and was about to give up the game, but his doctor persuaded him to kick a ball around a local park. Within days, thankfully, he was back at Old Trafford, determined to play in memory of his friends who had died at Munich. It didn't take long for Charlton to reach the footballing heights, for within a little over two months, he made his international debut against Scotland, marking the occasion with a spectacular goal.

By 1966 and the World Cup finals in England, Charlton's skills had reached their full maturity. He opened England's scoring against Mexico with a typical long-distance blast and went on to score some thrilling goals in the tournament, including both the goals in England's 2-1 semi-final win over Portugal. At the end of that season, he won both the Footballer of the Year and European player awards. In 1967, he won his third League Championship medal, though his finest moment was yet to come.

In May 1968, he scored two goals in the emotionally charged European Cup Final against Benfica of Portugal at Wembley, as United won 4-1. He walked off the pitch in tears; he had become one of the few footballers ever to achieve all their major ambitions. After 106 caps and 49 goals, his international career ended in Mexico in the 1970 World Cup in dramatic fashion. He was substituted in order to keep him fresh for the semi-finals as England led West Germany 2-0, but it wasn't to be, as the Germans ran out winners 3-2. In 1973, Bobby Charlton pulled on Manchester United's red jersey for the last time at Stamford Bridge. He had set appearance records for both club and country, scored a record 49 goals for England and become a footballing legend.

He joined Preston North End as manager and even played 38 games, but he didn't have the same level of success off the field and duly retired from management in 1975. He took up a position with a travel company as well as being an active director of Wigan Athletic, whom he managed for a brief spell at the end of the 1982-83 season.

MANCHESTER EVENING NEWS

He established the famous Bobby Charlton soccer schools for children, which have helped so many young players of all ages and abilities to improve their skills.

Manchester United honoured him with a place on the board. He had helped to make them the most famous club in the world and was one of the most talented and popular footballers of all time.

ALLENBY CHILTON

Birthplace:	South Hylton, Co Durham
Born:	16th September 1918
Position:	Centre-Half

Football League Career

	Appearances	Goals
Manchester United	352	3
Grimsby Town	63	0
Total	415	3

England International Appearances	2
Goals	0

Allenby Chilton arrived at Old Trafford in 1938 after a brief spell on trial with Liverpool. He had played junior football with Ford School, South Hylton, Sunderland Boys and Hylton Colliery Juniors, but it was from Seaham Colliery that he was signed in the November of that year. He was converted from wing-half to centre-half, prompting Louis Rocca, then United's chief scout and spotter of Chilton's talents, to predict, "This lad will be an international."

He made his debut for United on 2nd September 1939 against Charlton Athletic at The Valley. War was declared the next day and so he had to wait a further seven years before playing a League game against Grimsby Town in August 1946. It was unfortunate for Chilton, for like so many other footballers of his day, his career was shortened by the war, for his total of games played would have been much greater.

Despite being wounded while on service in Normandy, he guested for Charlton Athletic in wartime football, and won a Wartime South Cup winners' medal when 85,000 fans saw the men from The Valley beat Chelsea at Wembley.

As a young player, Chilton received plenty of crowd abuse, but he took it all in his stride, buckled down to the business of professional football and went on to make a big name for himself with the Reds. There was a time, though, that Allenby Chilton gave up football to try boxing, but after six months in the ring, he returned to soccer with no regrets whatsoever.

Throughout his career, he only scored three goals; strangely enough they all came in drawn games. He represented England on two occasions, against Northern Ireland in 1950 and France in 1951.

A tall and powerful centre-half, Allenby Chilton was United's only ever-present when they won the League title in 1951-52.

Chilton was the backbone of the Reds' defence and succeeded Johnny Carey as club captain. When he lost his place in the United line-up to Mark Jones in February 1955, Chilton ended a run of 166 consecutive League appearances. It was a United record until Steve Coppell broke it during the 1980-81 season.

Chilton played in nearly 400 games for United, winning an F.A. Cup winners' medal in 1948 and League Championship medal in 1951-52. Leaving Old Trafford in March 1955, he became player-manager at Grimsby Town, inspiring them to the Division Three North title in 1955-56. He ended his playing career shortly afterwards, but continued as manager. He left Grimsby in 1959, before later assisting non-League Wigan Athletic and Hartlepool United.

MANCHESTER EVENING NEWS

ROY CLARKE

Birthplace:	Newport
Born:	1st June 1925
Position:	Winger

Football League Career

	Appearances	Goals
Caridff City	39	11
Manchester City	349	73
Stockport County	25	5
Total	413	89

Wales International Appearances	22
Goals	5

Born in Newport, South Wales, Roy Clarke's first taste of international recognition was as a member of the Welsh Schools Baseball team in 1939. During the Second World War, he worked in the coalmines, but managed to play football for a local side at the weekends. He later joined Cardiff City, for whom he made 39 appearances and scored 11 goals, before joining Manchester City. Roy Clarke holds the unique record of playing in three different divisions of the Football League in three consecutive League games! He played his last game for the Bluebirds, who were at the time Third Division Champions in their penultimate game of the 1946-47 season before he joined the Maine Road club. He played in City's last game of their Second Division promotion winning season against his home-town club, Newport County – a game in which George Smith scored all five goals as City beat the Welsh side 5-1. Clarke's next game was at the start of the 1947-48 campaign with City in the top flight. They beat Wolves 4-3 at Molineux with Roy Clarke hitting the winner.

He won his first international cap for Wales against England in 1948 and his last eight years later against Northern Ireland. He made 22 appearances for his country, scoring 5 goals.

Roy Clarke was a left-winger with a very powerful shot and scored many vital goals during his stay at Maine Road. He was instrumental in City getting to Wembley at the end of the 1954-55 campaign. He hit both goals in the 2-0 win at Kenilworth Road as City deposed of Luton Town in the Fifth round. He also hit the only goal of the semi-final against Sunderland at Villa Park, but unfortunately Newcastle beat them in the Final 3-1.

The following season though, he picked up an F.A. Cup winners' medal after City had beaten Birmingham 3-1.

His best season for City was 1956-57, when he scored 11 goals from his 40 appearances.

In September 1958, he moved on to nearby Stockport County on a free transfer, where he played a further 25 League games for the Edgeley Park outfit. He had played in 349 League games for Manchester City and scored 73 goals.

He returned to Maine Road in 1966 to run the City Social

Club. After twenty two years, he retired on 27th September 1988, with hundreds of friends and colleagues paying tribute to him in a farewell party at Maine Road.

MANCHESTER EVENING NEWS

RONNIE CLAYTON

Birthplace: Preston
Born: 5th August 1934
Position: Wing-Half

Football League Career

	Appearances	Goals
Blackburn Rovers	577 (2)	14
Total	577 (2)	14

England International Appearances	35
Goals	0

Born in Preston on 8th August 1934, Ronnie Clayton joined Blackburn Rovers in 1949, making his Football League debut at the age of 16 in the 1950-51 season. His early promise led the then Blackburn manager Jackie Bestall to predict an England future for the talented youngster. Clayton had natural leadership qualities which showed early in his career. In September 1955 he won his first Under-23 cap and a month later he appeared for the England 'B' team. In November of that year, he completed the international sequence when he made his debut for the full England team.

He was a tremendous driving force in Blackburn's promotion back to the First Division in 1957-58.

Clayton was an energetic wing-half, strong in the tackle and a brilliant timer of the ball in the air. He also liked to power forward and instigate attacking moves.

He provided Ewood supporters with many magic moments during his long career, but there are perhaps few to rival the moment he scored a vital equalising goal in an F.A. Cup tie against Liverpool just minutes after he had returned to the field from treatment to what turned out to be a chipped knee cap. It was during Rovers' promotion season of 1957-58 and Rovers had already seen off Rotherham, Everton and Cardiff. There was a full house at Ewood Park to see a tense cup-tie in which Liverpool went in at half-time one goal up. There were just ten minutes left when Clayton, Rovers' captain courageous, came back to the field after having touchline treatment. He was just in time to line up for a free kick awarded against Liverpool. Roy Vernon took it out on the right wing and lobbed it towards the far post, where Clayton, moving quicker than anyone else, flung himself forward to connect with his forehead and send the ball into the corner of the net. It completely changed the course of the game, for a minute later, Ally McLeod grabbed the winner. It wasn't until the following Monday that it was discovered that Clayton had in fact chipped his knee cap!

He appeared in the final stages of the 1958 World Cup in Sweden and succeeded Billy Wright as captain for the last five of his 35 England appearances. He lost favour with the England selectors and surprisingly didn't appear again for his country after 1960.

He continued to give good service for Blackburn and led

them to Wembley in 1960, only for them to lose 0-3 to Wolverhampton Wanderers.

Remaining loyal to what many would class an unfashionable club, Ronnie Clayton experienced the highs and lows, but always maintained the same level of enthusiasm and endeavour. As age began to slow down his legs, he moved to play at the heart of the Blackburn defence, where he became a very accomplished centre-back. It was Clayton's masterful reading of the game that provided the solid defensive platform for the team.

At the end of the 1968-69 season, he finally left Ewood Park to become player-manager at Morecambe. He returned to Ewood once more in December 1970 for a well-deserved testimonial, before returning to north-east Lancashire to team up with Great Harwood.

Throughout a career that spanned 19 seasons, Ronnie Clayton remained one of football's finest ambassadors. He was without doubt one of the greatest players ever to wear the Rovers' colours.

WALLY & HOWARD TALBOT PHOTOGRAPHY

RAY CLEMENCE

Birthplace: Skegness
Born: 5th August 1948
Position: Goalkeeper

Football League Career

	Appearances	Goals
Scunthorpe United	48	0
Liverpool	470	0
Tottenham Hotspur	240	0
Total	758	0

England International Appearances	61
Goals	0

It was Bill Shankly who paid Scunthorpe United £18,000 for the 19-year-old goalkeeper who had made 48 appearances for the Irons in the lower divisions. Shankly's assessment of the man was that he was possibly the most important factor in Liverpool's continued success throughout the decade of the Seventies. Indeed, Clemence only missed six matches during that period.

He had to wait two and a half seasons before clinching a place in the first team as Tommy Lawrence's consistent form kept him out.

Clemence immediately impressed with his safe handling and sharp reflexes. He got down quickly to low shots, knew when and when not to come off his line and had great positional sense. In his first full season, he conceded only 22 goals in 41 games, helping the Reds equal the First Division record of 24 in a season. In 1978-79, he went even better, only letting in 16 goals.

Of course, being behind one of the the world's best defences, he needed to have great powers of concentration. He was kept idle for long periods, not getting a touch of the ball. It was a measure of his greatness that when he did have to respond, he would produce a top-class save. Of lightweight build and very athletic, he was able to spring several feet into the air and claim the ball with a very safe pair of hands. He was also one of the first goalkeepers to act as a sweeper behind his defence, leaving his penalty area to cut out the long through ball. His world-class saves were many, but perhaps there were none more important than in the 1975-76 U.E.F.A. Cup away leg at Dynamo Dresden. He saved a penalty by diving full length to his right to reach a hard low shot and keep the tie goalless after ninety minutes.

One of the finest goalkeepers in the history of the game, he was unlucky to be around at the same time as Peter Shilton, for throughout his illustrious career at international level in which he won 61 caps, he was always vying for the No 1 jersey with Shilts.

In August 1981, he announced that he was looking for a new challenge, even though he was still at the top of his game, and he moved to Spurs. He had hardly missed a match throughout his time at Anfield and picked up more club honours than any other goalkeeper. He holds the record for consecutive first-team appearances by an English goalkeeper – 325. Soon after moving to Spurs, he announced his retirement from international football.

By 1987-88, after helping Spurs reach the F.A. Cup Final, his high level of performances was being affected by his injuries. He played in just 13 matches that season, taking his career total to a staggering 1,119 first-team games.

When Bobby Mimms joined Tottenham from Everton, Ray began helping on the coaching side, his goalkeeping days over.

Probably the best goalkeeper Liverpool ever had, his 23 seasons had brought him five League Championship medals, five F.A. Cup Final appearances, three European Cup winners' medals and an M.B.E. in the Queen's Birthday Honours for his services to football.

MANCHESTER EVENING NEWS

HENRY COCKBURN

Birthplace:	Ashton-under-Lyne
Born:	14th September 1923
Position:	Wing-Half

Football League Career

	Appearances	Goals
Manchester United	243	4
Bury	35	0
Total	278	4
England International Appearances		13
Goals		0

Born in Ashton-under-Lyne in 1923, Henry Cockburn joined Manchester United from a local junior club, Goslings, which was, at the time, a Reds' nursery club. He made his first-team debut for United in wartime football against Tranmere Rovers in 1943. He wore the number nine shirt as United won 6-3. The match was abandoned after 85 minutes, but the score stood.

He made his League debut in the opening match of the 1946-47 campaign against Grimsby Town, the Reds running out winners 2-1. He won the first of his international caps after only six League games, although it should be said that the League proper had only just restarted after the war. He went on to win 13 full caps for England, completing quite a formidable international half-back line with Stoke City's centre-half Neil Franklin and Wolves' Billy Wright. He played his last match for England against France in 1951. He also represented the Football League and collected a 'B' cap. Though he was a dapper little player, standing only 5ft 4ins tall, he was certainly not too small and fragile for the hectic battle of League and International football.

He was a great player in a club side because he worked so hard for the team and his enthusiasm rubbed off on to other people. His positional play was so good, he never failed – he always wanted to win.

Henry Cockburn was one of the finest wing-halves in the English game. Lack of height and weight was no handicap, for his timing was perfect and he could outjump players much taller than himself. One of the most astute ball players that Manchester United have ever had on their books, he played his final League game for the Reds on 2nd October 1954 against Wolverhampton Wanderers.

He won an F.A. Cup winners' medal in 1948 and a League Championship medal in 1951-52. After playing in 275 games for Manchester United, he left to join near neighbours Bury, where he played in 35 League games before signing for Peterborough United, who were then in the Midland League. He then had spells with other non-League clubs, Corby Town and Sankeys (Wellington) before he returned to the Football League as assistant-trainer to Oldham Athletic in 1961.

His final move took him to Huddersfield Town, where he became coach under another Man-chester United old boy,

Ian Greaves.
A terrier, Henry Cockburn would run for ninety minutes and wouldn't give the opposition anything.

MANCHESTER EVENING NEWS

JOHN CONNELLY

Birthplace: St Helens
Born: 18th July 1938
Position: Winger

Football League Career

	Appearances	Goals
Burnley	215	86
Manchester United	79 (1)	22
Blackburn Rovers	148 (1)	36
Bury	128	37
Total	570 (2)	181

England International Appearances	20
Goals	7

On leaving school at the age of 15, John Connelly worked as an apprentice joiner, but as the school team he played for joined the St Helens J.O.L. League, he continued to play for them. At 16 years of age, he played as an inside-left for St Helens Town in the Lancashire Combination, his first match being against Burscough. He signed for Burnley in 1956, but remained as an amateur until he had completed his apprenticeship as a joiner at the age of 21. He made his debut for Burnley in his first season at Turf Moor against Leeds United and signed as a full-time professional at 22 years of age. It was immaterial as to which flank the notably two-footed Connelly occupied. He was direct and always seeking to have a shot on goal. He was one of the top scoring wingmen in the game throughout the late fifties and early sixties.

He was a member of the Turf Moor club's Championship winning side of 1959-60, scoring 20 goals in 34 games. In his time at Burnley, he was selected for the England Under-23 team and played his first international game for the full England side against Wales at Cardiff. He also appeared in the 1962 F.A. Cup Final when Burnley lost to Spurs. He made 215 League appearances and scored 86 goals before joining Manchester United for £60,000 in April 1964.

He made his United debut in the 2-2 home draw against West Bromwich Albion at the start of the 1964-65 season. He scored 15 goals that campaign, helping United to win the Championship and thus collect his second Championship medal. He hammered in one of the goals on March 9th 1966 as the much-vaunted 'Eagles of Lisbon' Benfica had been completely outplayed and beaten 5-1 by United.

He last appeared for England in the opening match of the 1966 World Cup Finals in a goalless draw with Uruguay. He played 20 times for England and scored 7 goals.

After two years at Old Trafford, where he scored 35 goals in his 113 first-team appearances, he left United for £40,000, going to play for Blackburn Rovers.

He continued to find the net, scoring 36 goals in 149 League games for Blackburn, a good striking rate for a winger.

He ended his Football League career at Gigg Lane, making 128 League appearances for the Shakers before retiring in 1972 to take over a fish and chip shop.

MANCHESTER EVENING NEWS

STEVE COPPELL

Birthplace:	Liverpool
Born:	9th July 1955
Position:	Forward

Football League Career

	Appearances	Goals
Tranmere Rovers	35 (3)	10
Manchester United	320 (2)	54
Total	355 (5)	64

England International Appearances	42
Goals	7

Steve Coppell's football career didn't conform to the normal pattern from schoolboy forms through apprentice professional to the full-time player. He was always considered too small to be a successful footballer when at school. He was studying economics at Liverpool University and in his first year, when Tranmere Rovers rated him highly enough to play him as an amateur in their Third Division side. He made his League debut for Tranmere Rovers at Prenton Park in January 1974 in the match against Aldershot. After 38 games for Tranmere his enormous potential was spotted by then top of the Second Division Manchester United and in February 1975, he was signed by Tommy Docherty for a fee of £30,000. It was the time when wingers were just coming back into fashion and Coppell became one of the new breed of wide midfield players. Manager Docherty later enthused that Steve Coppell was his best ever signing.

Coppell established himself in United's first team almost at once and progressed to international level almost immediately. He appeared once in the England Under-23 side, before making his full international debut against Italy in 1977.

Steve Coppell could wriggle past defenders, race to the line and send over a perfect cross, but he could also chase back and provide cover for his defenders. He also had a knack of cutting in from the right flank and hitting some waist high drives.

He gained an F.A. Cup winners' medal in 1977 and appeared in over 400 competitive games for the Reds, including the 1983 Milk Cup Final. Not a particularly noted goalscorer, he ended the 1978-79 season as joint-top scorer with 11 goals. Noted for his all-action, never-say-die attitude, his career was brought to an early end by a tackle from the Hungarian defender Joseph Toth at Wembley in November 1981.

He struggled on for another 14 months, producing some of his best ever football and undergoing three operations, but there was no way back. He was able to play in the first four games of the 1982 World Cup finals, but the problem flared up again in the goalless draw against West Germany. He managed to play two more games for England to end with 42 caps, finishing eight short of his personal target of 50 caps. He was forced to retire from playing on medical advice following this serious knee injury. He had enjoyed just ten years at the top, but had made quite an impression.

In June 1984, he turned to management with Crystal Palace, showing the same enthusiasm that he did while Chairman of the Professional Footballers' Association, making him at 28, the youngest League manager. Steve Coppell was respected by his fellow footballers not only for his great skill as a winger but for his integrity and intelligent views on the game.

MANCHESTER EVENING NEWS

JOE CORRIGAN

Birthplace: Manchester
Born: 18th November 1948
Position: Goalkeeper

Football League Career

	Appearances	Goals
Manchester City	476	0
Brighton Hove Albion	36	0
Norwich City	3	0
Stoke City	9	0
Total	524	0

England International Appearances	9
Goals	0

Born in Manchester, Joe Corrigan joined Manchester City as a junior in 1966, when he was playing for Sale Football Club. After being singled out in club trials, where he gave some impressive performances, he turned professional at Maine Road in January 1967.

His first-team debut for Manchester City was in the League Cup tie against Blackpool at Maine Road, which ended at 1-1 in October of the same year. He had to wait until March 1969 for his Football League debut at Portman Road, Ipswich beating City 2-1.

In his early days, he was always in the shadow of Harry Dowd and Ken Mulhearn, though when he did get a get a chance, he was inconsistent. Despite this unimpressive start to his League career, he fought hard to establish himself, but faced another crisis of confidence when in 1975, City signed Keith MacRae for £100,000 from Motherwell. Out of favour with the then City manager Ron Saunders, he asked for a transfer and was transfer-listed in February 1974. However, once again the 6ft 4 $^{1}/_{2}$ins goalkeeper buckled down and won back his first-team place, going on to serve City for a further nine years. Manchester City have had three outstanding goalkeepers since the war – Swift, Trautmann, and Corrigan was the third. I'm sure if he'd been around at a different time than Ray Clemence and Peter Shilton, he would have collected far more than the nine caps he did win. He won his first in 1976, coming on as substitute against Italy in New York and his last against Iceland in 1982. He also played in an unofficial international for England against Athletico Bilbao in 1981, plus ten appearances for England 'B'.

His best season for City was 1976-77 when he only conceded 34 goals in his 42 League appearances, keeping 22 clean sheets.

He won League Cup honours in 1970 and 1976 and a European Cup winners' medal in 1970 when City beat Gornik Zabrze 2-1. When City played Tottenham Hotspur at Wembley in the 1981 F.A. Cup Final, Corrigan had looked unbeatable – the game ending at 1-1. For his heroics between the posts, Corrigan was named man-of-

MANCHESTER EVENING NEWS

the-match, though he was beaten three times in the replay, as the North London side won 3-2.

Corrigan played in 476 League games for Manchester City and in another 116 in other Cup matches, making him second only to Alan Oakes in terms of the number of first-team games for City. In March 1983, City transferred him to Seattle Sounders in the N.A.S.L. for £30,000. He later returned to these shores to play 48 games for Brighton and Hove Albion, Norwich City and Stoke City, before retiring.

PAT CRERAND

Birthplace:	Glasgow	
Born:	19th February 1939	
Position:	Wing-Half	

Football League Career

	Appearances	Goals
Manchester United	304	10
Total	304	10

England International Appearances	16
Goals	0

A pupil at St Luke's School in the Gorbals District of Glasgow, Pat Crerand started his career as a footballer with Duntocher Hibs in 1957 and signed professional forms for Celtic in 1958. He won a Scottish Cup winners' medal with one of the most successful clubs north of the border. In his time at Parkhead, he was capped 11 times by Scotland, collected one Under-23 cap and represented the Scottish League.

Transferred to Manchester United on 6th February 1963 for £56,000, he quickly made himself a favourite with the Old Trafford crowd. After only a few months with United, he won an F.A. Cup winners' medal in the 3-1 defeat of Leicester City. His transfer to United was, at the time, a record transfer fee for a wing-half.

Crerand was a thoughtful player with a firm belief in attacking, constructive football; he initiated numerous attacks with long, shrewd passes. His strong, compact build gave him scope to tackle swiftly and firmly – and began to give United a much more balanced look. Any lack of pace was certainly more than compensated for by his superb distribution skills. 'Paddy' Crerand was an architect, sweeping out accurate crossfield passes of 40 and 50 yards from midfield to his forwards.

Along with Bobby Charlton and Nobby Stiles, he formed the midfield that drove Manchester United to victory in the European Cup. He also went on to collect two Championship medals in 1965 and 1967, his creative skills being a big factor behind United's success throughout the 1960s.

After United's 4-3 win at Maine Road in the final game of the 1970-71 season, Crerand decided to retire. He had played in 392 first-team games for the Reds and though he only scored 15 goals, he made many more. One of his goals came in the 5-1 hammering of Benfica in Lisbon, as he pounced on Denis Law's defence-splitting pass.

One of Manchester United's most cheerful jokers, Pat Crerand was deadly serious on the field, always giving 100% effort. It was always said that, "When Crerand's playing well, so are United." He joined the coaching staff at Old Trafford in August 1971 before, in January 1973, becoming assistant manager.

He left Manchester in July 1976 to become manager at Northampton Town where he stayed for six months, before leaving the game to run a public house.

Of Irish descent, Paddy Crerand was one of the most constructive wing-halves of the 1960s.

MANCHESTER EVENING NEWS

KENNY DALGLISH

Birthplace: Glasgow
Born: 4th March 1951
Position: Midfield; Forward

Football League Career

	Appearances	Goals
Liverpool	342 (16)	118
Total	342 (16)	118

Scotland International Appearances	102
Goals	30

Brought up in the shadow of Ibrox Park, it was always assumed that Kenny Dalglish would play in the blue of Rangers and not the green and white hoops. But it was Celtic who signed him. When their assistant manager Sean Fallon went to meet the family, the young Dalglish rushed around in a panic ripping the Rangers pictures off the wall in the living room.

He had been spotted playing for Glasgow United, the best boys' team in Scotland, and had already won two Scottish Under-15 caps. The top English clubs, including Liverpool, were also interested, but Celtic loaned him to Cumbernauld United, while he worked as a joiner and shopfitter. He made his first-team debut for Celtic on 4th October 1969 against Raith Rovers. In his first full season with Celtic, Dalglish scored 17 goals and made his international debut as substitute in Scotland's 1-0 win over Belgium in 1971.

His skills were subtle and stemmed from the balance and speed with which he controlled the ball. His passing was immaculate and his deceptive swirls in full flight would often send defenders the wrong way.

In his eight years with Celtic, he won five League titles, four Scottish Cups and a Scottish League Cup winners' medal. In his final season at Parkhead, he led them to yet another League and Cup double, this time as captain. Celtic manager Jock Stein recognised Dalglish's all-round skills and assigned him to midfield, where he still continued to score memorable goals. On being asked Kenny's best position, Jock Stein replied, "Och, just let him on the park."

By the age of 26, Dalglish wanted to prove himself in England and in 1977, Liverpool signed him for £440,000, manager Bob Paisley citing the player's 'attitude' – his dedication, professionalism and determination to succeed – as his reasons for wanting the Scot at Anfield.

He made a quiet start in the Charity Shield against Manchester United, but scored on his League debut at Middlesbrough. He ended his first season as top scorer as Liverpool stormed to the League title again and Dalglish was voted Footballer of the Year.

After joining Liverpool, he made 177 consecutive League and Cup appearances before missing his first game in 1980. That was the year he picked up another European

Cup winners' medal and Liverpool retained their League title.
He had been instrumental in Liverpool winning the 1978 European Cup Final against Bruges. He scored the only goal of the game – a chip that dribbled into the far corner after Dalglish had waited for the Belgian 'keeper to commit himself. He played in the World Cup Finals of 1974, 1978 and 1982. In Argentina in 1978, he scored the equaliser in Scotland's famous 3-2 win over Holland.
Liverpool continued to dominate British football and Dalglish was a key figure. In 1983, he scored his 100th goal for Liverpool to become only the third player ever to score a century of goals in both Scottish and English football. He was also voted Footballer of the Year again and picked up the players' 'Player of the Year' award as the Reds won their fourteenth championship.
The tragedy at the 1985 European Cup Final brought an end to the Reds' international triumphs. The deaths of 38 fans at the Heysel Stadium in Brussels led to the banning of English clubs from all European competitions. Shortly after this, Dalglish was appointed as successor to Joe Fagan as Liverpool manager.
His first season in charge could not have been more successful. Liverpool became only the third club this century to win the League and F.A. Cup double, with Kenny's goal at Stamford Bridge clinching the championship. Not only did Dalglish win the Manager of the Year award, but he collected his 100th cap.
He failed to reach the required fitness standards and was forced to withdraw from Scotland's 1986 World Cup squad. He bowed out of Scotland's national team with great pride, having scored 30 goals (joint-top with Law) in 102 appearances – he had become the only Scottish footballer to play more than a century of matches for his country.
Tragedy struck his career again in April 1989 when 95 Liverpool fans died at Hillsborough. By then, Kenny Dalglish had become manager and continued to have great success until 22nd February 1991 when he rocked the soccer world by resigning as manager of Liverpool, citing the pressures of the job. The annnouncement came just two days after the 4-4 draw in the F.A. Cup fifth-round replay against Everton, acclaimed as one of the best Merseyside derby games of all time.

LIVERPOOL DAILY POST & ECHO

WYN DAVIES

Birthplace: Caernarvon
Born: 20th March 1942
Position: Centre-Forward

Football League Career

	Appearances	Goals
Wrexham	55	22
Bolton Wanderers	155	66
Newcastle United	181	40
Manchester City	45	8
Manchester United	15 (1)	4
Blackpool	34 (2)	5
Crystal Palace	3	0
Stockport County	28 (2)	7
Crewe Alexandra	50 (5)	13
Total	566 (10)	165
Wales International Appearances		34
Goals		7

As a boy, Wyn Davies considered himself an average parks player, yet he was to develop into one of the finest headers of the ball in post-war soccer.

Born in Caernarvon, he began his career with Llanberis Juniors before joining his home-town club, Caernarvon Town. From there, he went into the League with Wrexham, signing professional forms in July 1961. He developed his scoring talents at the Racecourse Ground, scoring 22 goals in 55 appearances. This prompted Bolton Wanderers to pay £20,000 for him in March 1962, Wrexham taking Ernie Phythian in exchange. He was quickly installed into the Wanderers' number nine shirt and made 12 appearances towards the end of the 1961-62 season, scoring three goals. Except for periods of injury, he was a Bolton regular for four and a half years. In September 1964, he hit the first of three hat-tricks for the Wanderers in a 3-0 win over Southampton at Burnden Park.

In 1964, he won the first of his Welsh caps and was capped 16 times in his days as a Bolton player. In 1964-65, he was Bolton's top scorer with 25 League and Cup goals. 'Wyn the Leap', as he was affectionately known, made an explosive start to the 1966-67 campaign, scoring 12 times in his first 12 League games, including two hat-tricks against Carlisle United and Preston North End.

Bolton were then in the Second Division and Wyn's name became linked with almost every First Division club. In October 1966, when Newcastle United made a bid of £80,000 for him, he took the chance to return to the First Division with them.

Davies was a member of the Magpies' 1969 Fairs Cup-winning team and after scoring 46 goals in 187 appearances, he returned to the north-west with Manchester City.

He certainly moved about during his career and some thirteen months later, he joined arch-rivals Manchester United. He then had spells at Blackpool, Crystal Palace

and Stockport County before finishing his League career at Crewe Alexandra in the summer of 1979.
His amazing heading talents in the centre-forward position have thrilled the crowds wherever he has played. He collected 34 Welsh caps in a career spanning 18 years.
He spent some time with Arcadia Shepherds F.C. in South Africa before returning to his native North Wales with Bangor City and England full-back Chris Lawler.

MANCHESTER EVENING NEWS

TOMMY DOCHERTY

Birthplace:	Glasgow
Born:	24th August 1928
Position:	Wing-Half

Football League Career

	Appearances	Goals
Preston North End	324	5
Arsenal	83	1
Chelsea	4	0
Total	411	6

Scotland International Appearances	25
Goals	1

No fanfares greeted the Glasgow-born Tommy Docherty when he arrived at Deepdale from Celtic on 5th November 1949 for £4,000 – he wasn't even first reserve.

His North End debut on Christmas Eve 1949 hardly created a ripple, for starting at outside-left, he was dropped. He deputised for Tom Finney in a farcical Cup replay won by Watford, but was again dropped. Soon, he got in at right-half and was never dropped again. He was fast and tigerish and could tear apart assaults with demoralising abruptness. A fearless wing-half, he was capable of dispossessing the smartest of opponents and instantly turning defence into attack with the drive of an aggressive ball player. A terror in the tackle, he was certainly no angel, but his tackling in the main was fair. 'The Doc' had the cure for most inside-forwards – they were never keen on a second visit!

Preston manager Cliff Britton bowed to Docherty's persistent and mystifying requests for a transfer; he left for Arsenal for £28.000 in August 1958. He had made 324 of a possible 356 League appearances for Preston. He missed 21 through injury and seven through being called upon by Scotland.

Tragically ironic for Docherty was his misfortune in breaking a leg when playing for the Gunners against Preston.

He packed away his boots to accept the post of senior coach to Chelsea. During an emergency, Docherty played four League games for Chelsea before being appointed caretaker-manager in September 1961 when Ted Drake parted company with the club. Four months later, his appointment was confirmed on a firm basis. Under his guidance, the young Chelsea side reached the F.A. Cup semi-final three seasons in succession, going to Wembley in 1967, only to lose to Spurs 2-1.

One of the game's most controversial characters, he was an outspoken and much travelled manager. I feel it is worth chronicling his exploits. He left Chelsea in November 1967 and within a few weeks took over as Rotherham's chief. After a year at Millmoor, he took on the challenge at Queen's Park Rangers, but after a disagreement on policy, he left within a month. He was due to take over as team-chief to Athletico Bilbao in Spain, but before he went, the Aston Villa directors asked him to help them out.

After a spell with Porto, he was appointed Scotland's team manager in 1971, giving them an immediate boost before succeeding Frank O'Farrell at Old Trafford.

In his four and a half seasons with United, he assembled an exciting side. In 1977, he made his 8th appearance at Wembley as a player and a manager, but his first as a winner. Docherty was dismissed later that year and with his United job went his best chance of major managerial success.

In July 1981, he was back in Lancashire soccer, as manager of the Deepdale club where he'd made his name, after coaching in Australia for twelve months.

Now a popular radio celebrity with Piccadilly, he gets the same response from the listeners as he did from the players in his charge at Old Trafford. As a player 'Doc' was undoubtedly one of the game's great characters.

WALLY & HOWARD TALBOT PHOTOGRAPHY

BRYAN DOUGLAS

Birthplace: Blackburn
Born: 27th May 1934
Position: Inside-Forward; Winger

Football League Career

	Appearances	Goals
Blackburn Rovers	438	102
Total	438	102
England International Appearances		36
Goals		11

Bryan Douglas' only ambition as a youngster was to wear the blue and white of Blackburn Rovers. Practically living on the doorstep of Ewood Park, he joined his home town team as a groundstaff boy in 1952, after he had much success with Blackburn Schoolboys.

Unfortunately for Bryan and Blackburn, National Service disrupted his early career and he did not make his first-team debut until 1954. During those early days in the team, he was often criticised for being over-elaborate and too selfish. Deceptively frail-looking at 5ft 6ins, he was later to confound those critics and become one of England's greatest post-war footballers.

He had helped Blackburn to win promotion from Division Two in 1957-58, when they finished one point behind West Ham United. That was the season he made his England debut against Wales, wearing Stanley Matthews' number seven shirt. Considering that Douglas played in the era of Finney, Matthews, Charlton, Haynes and Greaves, he did well to play for his country so often. In fact, he won 36 caps and scored 11 goals – an excellent return for a winger. Blackburn preferred to use him as a scheming inside-forward. He hit his passes beautifully and used to sit in the centre of midfield knocking the ball around.

One of the days to be remembered in Rovers' history was the day that manager Johnny Carey switched Douglas to outside-right as Roy Vernon went away to do his National Service. The Rovers romped home against a poor Bury side at Gigg Lane 4-0 with Douglas scoring the third after cheekily walking round goalkeeper Conway.

Bryan Douglas had the most perfect close control it is possible to see. His shuffling feet carved up opposing defences for more than a decade during which he made a succession of forwards, notably Fred Pickering and Peter McEvoy, into frequent goalscorers with his inch-perfect passes. On a muddy Upton Park pitch in 1963-64, he was the executioner-in-chief as Pickering and McEvoy both claimed hat-tricks as Blackburn beat West Ham 8-2.

Probably the two high points in Bryan's distinguished career were playing in the 1960 F.A. Cup Final, where Rovers lost 3-0 to Wolves and then playing in all four of England's games in the 1962 World Cup in Chile. A cartilage operation, coupled with other injuries, meant that he missed most of Blackburn's struggle against relegation in 1965-66. The 1966-67 season was his last as a truly effective member of the Rovers first-team squad, as his final years at Ewood were dogged by injury. He finally retired from the first-class game at the end of the 1968-69 season and spent a couple of seasons playing non-League football for Great Harwood with Ronnie Clayton and Roy Vernon.

A brilliant ball-playing forward, Bryan Douglas made up for a lack of height and physical strength with great vision and artistry.

MANCHESTER EVENING NEWS

MIKE DOYLE

Birthplace: Manchester
Born: 25th November 1946
Position: Midfield; Defender

Football League Career

	Appearances	Goals
Manchester City	441 (7)	32
Stoke City	115	5
Bolton Wanderers	40	2
Rochdale	24	1
Total	620 (7)	40

England International Appearances	5
Goals	0

Mike Doyle was a very determined player in whatever position he was given. Born in Manchester, he played for Stockport Boys before joining the Maine Road groundstaff in 1962.

He made his first-team debut for Manchester City as a centre-forward against Cardiff City on 12th March 1965, after giving impressive displays for the Youth and Central League side. He went on to make more than 500 first-team appearances for City in either midfield or defence. It was his influence during the 1965-66 season that went a long way in helping City get out of the Second Division. Certainly not a prolific goalscorer, when he did score, they were usually important goals. He scored six goals in a four-match spell over the Christmas period that season to help consolidate City's position at the top of the division. He was also instrumental in City topping the First Division in 1968. It was during this season that he played in his first representative game, playing for the England Under-23s against Hungary and for Young England against an England XI. There followed appearances for the Football League, the first in 1972 against the Scottish League. Doyle seemed to save his goals for the European competitions or for the domestic trophy finals.

He scored the equalising goal at Wembley in the 1970 League Cup Final after West Bromwich Albion had gone a goal up, City going on to lift the trophy after Glyn Pardoe had hit the winner. In April 1970, he scored one of the goals in the European Cup-winners' semi-final second leg against Schalke 04, City winning 5-1 after losing by the only goal in Germany.

The following month he had an outstanding first-half against Gornik Zabrze in Vienna, as City won their first European trophy. The Maine Road side had gone into half-time two goals ahead and though they conceded a goal in the 68th minute after Doyle had gone off with an injured ankle, they hung on. He also scored against the Polish side in the 1970-71 Cup Winners' cup campaign. Doyle scored to make it 2-2 on aggregate and force a third match, which City won 3-1 in Copenhagen. Unfortunately, City lost to Chelsea in the two-legged Final with Doyle missing both matches due to injury. Mike Doyle was one of City's finest players under Mercer and Allison and later Tony Book, winning two League Cup winners' medals, an F.A. Cup winners' medal and a European Cup winners' medal.

After Rodney Marsh left Maine Road in 1975, he was made club captain and a year later made the first of his five full international appearances for England against Wales.

After struggling to get back into the City side after injury, he was transferred to Stoke City for £50,000 in June 1978 and played over 100 games for the Potters. He later played for both Bolton and Rochdale before retiring.

MANCHESTER EVENING NEWS

TONY DUNNE

Birthplace:	Dublin
Born:	24th July 1941
Position:	Full-Back

Football League Career

	Appearances	Goals
Manchester United	415	2
Bolton Wanderers	166 (4)	0
Total	581 (4)	2

Republic of Ireland International Appearances	32
Goals	0

Tony Dunne's career began as a centre-forward with St Finbar's and Tara United in the Republic of Ireland. When he moved to Manchester United in August 1960, he cost the Reds just £5,000. He made his United debut at Burnley in October of that year, the first of 415 League appearances for the Old Trafford outfit.

A full-back whose speed, finesse and anticipation made up for what he lacked in size, he was small though compact and quick on the turn. Dunne was a calm, determined defender, often showing a willingness to move up into attack to put over crosses like a first-class winger. He gained two League Championship medals with United in 1965 and 1967 and an F.A. Cup winners' medal in 1963. In 1968, he won a European Cup winners' medal as United beat Benfica 4-1 at Wembley.

He was first capped for his country under his former Manchester United team-mate, Johnny Giles. He gained 32 caps and was voted Ireland's Footballer of the Year in 1969, an honour which he thoroughly deserved.

Dunne was tagged the quiet man during his United days. He was in the same United team as George Best, Bobby Charlton, Denis Law, Nobby Stiles and Pat Crerand – what else could he be? Dunne was just happy to stay in the background and line up alongside these great names on match days.

His career at Old Trafford ended in August 1973, when he joined Bolton Wanderers on a free transfer. He was 32 years of age when he arrived at Burnden Park and after a rather indifferent start, he settled down to become the regular left-back for the Trotters for five seasons, proving to be a bargain capture. He played in 170 League games for the Wanderers without scoring a goal, though he had managed two for United. He was a member of the Bolton team that won promotion to the First Division in 1978 and one of his final games in the top flight came at Old Trafford in April 1979, when the Wanderers won 2-1. He was one of the last playing survivors of the all-conquering Manchester United side of the 1960s.

He retired at the end of that season, after having won a further six caps at international level.

He moved to America in 1979, but he wasn't away from Burnden Park for long, returning as coach before becoming chief coach to Wanderers' boss Stan Anderson in 1980. He finally left Burnden in April 1981 when George Mulhall rejoined the club as assistant manager.

MANCHESTER EVENING NEWS

BILL ECKERSLEY

Birthplace:	Southport
Born:	16th July 1925
Position:	Full-Back

Football League Career

	Appearances	Goals
Blackburn Rovers	407	21
Total	407	21

England International Appearances	17
Goals	0

Bill Eckersley was an ex-lorry driver from Southport who might never have played for Blackburn Rovers if they hadn't been a man short for an 'A' team fixture at Feniscowles. He got to play in borrowed boots with string for shoelaces and only a couple of studs on each boot! What a player he was, joining the Rovers in November 1947 at a time when the club were struggling to recover from the repercussions of war.

In the last game of the 1947-48 campaign, the Rovers, who were already doomed to relegation, gave him a first-team chance. In the course of the next few seasons, he matured into the club's outstanding player after quickly establishing himself in the first team.

Though lacking in height and weight (he was so small he could stand under a table!) his tackling was keen and he had a tremendous amount of composure and style. He was a most constructive and attacking full-back. He had the clever knack of making a winger go the way he wanted to and though he was aggressive, he could be very subtle too when required. Bill's distribution was first-class but, unlike some of today's full-backs, he made sure he did his defensive job first. He gained selection for England regularly as Alf Ramsey's partner, winning 17 caps between 1950 and 1953. Perhaps he should have had a lot more for he was extremely tenacious, very fit and quick. Despite his success on the international scene, club honours eluded him. A number of promotion near-misses and two F.A. Cup semi-finals were all that was achieved during his prime. Unfortunately for Bill, his career was coming to an end when promotion was finally achieved in 1958. He was plagued by injuries and missed the 1960 F.A. Cup run. As club captain, he led the side by example on the field, whilst off it, his sharp sense of humour kept the dressing-room morale high. He was completely immune to the pressures that the game brought. When he was confronted with a last minute penalty in an F.A. Cup tie against West Bromwich Albion, he not only dealt with the goalkeeper's gamesmanship, but topped it with a smiling retort before smashing the ball into the back of the net!

During his final two seasons, he only made a handful of appearances – it was a crying shame that the knee injury came along to close his career. He retired in 1961 and a crowd of 21,000 turned up to pay him an emotional farewell at Ewood in his testimonial.

Unfortunately, his life outside the game wasn't kind to him and a confectionery business he ran near Ewood wasn't a success. He returned to driving during his later days, before he died at the tragically early age of 54.

A player of limitless talent, his ashes were scattered on the Ewood turf by his sons Billy and Stephen in an emotional ceremony before a first-team game.

LANCASHIRE EVENING TELEGRAPH

DUNCAN EDWARDS

Birthplace:	Dudley
Born:	1st October 1936
Died:	21st February 1958
Position:	Wing-Half

Football League Career

	Appearances	Goals
Manchester United	151	19
Total	151	19

England International Appearances	18
Goals	5

Born in Dudley, Worcestershire, Duncan Edwards played for the town's boys team at the age of 11 – the average age of the team was 15! He also played for the Birmingham and District Schools team and it was on Birmingham City's ground in May 1952, that Manchester United's assistant manager, Jimmy Murphy, persuaded him to join the Reds. Then 16 and captain of his county as a schoolboy, he had been snatched from under the noses of several Midlands clubs who had watched the young giant's progress with great interest. Two hours after his 16th birthday, Matt Busby went personally to the youngster's home to sign him for United.

Once at Old Trafford, he soon impressed, making an immediate impact in the newly launched F.A. Youth Cup in 1952-53. He played a big part in helping United establish themselves as the masters of the Youth Cup, as they won the competition for five successive seasons from its inception – Edwards playing in the first three.

At the age of 16 years 185 days, he was plunged, without any qualms on the part of Matt Busby, into League football when he made his debut against Cardiff City on 4th April 1953.

On the international front, he was the youngest to play for England when given his first cap in April 1955 at the age of 18 years 183 days. He starred in a 7-2 triumph over Scotland at Wembley, which was also a record at the time. He won 18 full caps and in addition, he won four England 'B' caps and hit six goals in one of his six matches at Under-23 level as he played up front.

By the time he had reached 20, he was controlling games to such an extent, that people were hailing him as the most complete footballer of any era and he scored unforgettable goals, not only for Manchester United, but also for England. So typical of them were his first and his last in the League. When he hit the first at Old Trafford, everybody it seemed had turned up to see the old maestro, Stanley Matthews, playing that day for Blackpool. Edwards too, was as thrilled as anybody about the presence of the man who was his soccer idol.

But it was Duncan who triggered off the crowd's roars with a superb sample of his skill when he steered a dipping shot over the head of goalkeeper George Farm.

His last goal, only days before disaster struck, was at Highbury, when he left Arsenal fans with the memory of a bullet-like drive that ripped home from 25 yards.

After England had beaten West Germany 3-1 in the Olympic Stadium in Berlin in 1956, he became known as 'Boom Boom' for his shots were packed with so much power. Receiving the ball on the left of his own penalty box from 'keeper Reg Matthews, he beat one man and advanced to the halfway line. He beat another, then three more inside the German half and then from fully 30 yards out, hit a left-footer into the roof of the net like a rocket.

'Big Dunk' was the golden youth who could well have become the greatest soccer immortal of them all, had his football not been denied to all supporters before he had barely started living. The tragic air crash at Munich in February 1958 not only crushed the might of a fine Manchester United side, but denied the Black Country boy's dreams – a boy so dedicated to the game he loved.

MANCHESTER EVENING NEWS

After 15 days of fighting valiantly for his life as he had fought on a football field, this soccer prodigy died. He was only 21 and on the threshold of what surely would have been a magnificent career. Today he is remembered in his home town of Dudley in the West Midlands, by a stained glass window at St Francis's Church.

MIKE ENGLAND

Birthplace:	Holywell
Born:	2nd December 1941
Position:	Centre-Half; Wing-Half; Centre-Forward

Football League Career

	Appearances	Goals
Blackburn Rovers	165	21
Tottenham Hotspur	300	14
Cardiff City	40	1
Total	505	36

Wales International Appearances	44
Goals	3

A member of Blackburn Rovers' F.A. Youth Cup winning side of 1959, he went on to become possibly the finest centre-half of his generation. He came into the Blackburn side of Ronnie Clayton and Bryan Douglas in its declining years. A natural athlete, England was capable of playing in a variety of positions. In fact, due to the consistency of Matt Woods, England's early first-team appearances were often at full-back or wing-half. He only appeared at centre-half when Woods was injured.

He quickly matured into an outstanding defender and was installed as the first-choice centre-half at the start of the 1963-64 season. His vision on the field and his ability to read the game rivalled that of the most constructive of midfield players.

England's height made him dominant in the air, whilst on the ground, his speed and strength made him the most daunting of defenders for the quickest of opposition forwards. Yet his game wasn't just based on power. For such a big man, he had the deftest of touches and his instant control and superb distribution put him on a par with the greatest defenders of all-time. Although a centre-half (a position in which he excelled) he was equally at home as an attacking wing-half or at centre-forward, where he played very successfully for Blackburn. He was a stubborn and fiercely ambitious player and when Rovers initially refused to allow him to try his luck with a bigger club, he threatened to quit the game altogether. However, his restless ambition to play for a big city club wasn't contained, when after holding out for several months in a one-man rebellion, he signed a one year's contract with Rovers. It was said in many quarters that Blackburn was a soccer backwater and the poor home gates couldn't be conducive to encouraging anyone to think that the town was going to see a big soccer revival. When Rovers were relegated in 1965-66, it became obvious that they would now have to sell their most viable asset and though England was linked with Manchester United, it was to White Hart Lane that he went. The fee for England was £95,000, which was a record sum for a defender at the time.

Bill Nicholson, the then Spurs manager said, "I signed

him because he liked heading the ball and that's the major part of the job for a player in that position." England was a key element in the rebuilding of the Tottenham side following the break-up of the legendary double team. His influence was immediate, as Spurs won the F.A. Cup in 1967, the League Cup in 1971, the U.E.F.A. Cup in 1972 and the League Cup again in 1973. Already a regular on the international scene in his days at Ewood, he went on to win 44 caps for Wales as well as 11 Under-23 caps. Disheartened by Tottenham's abrupt decline, he decided to retire. His decision I feel was a hasty one and after a brief summer in America, he returned to play 40 games for Cardiff City, helping them win promotion from Division Three, before returning to the States.

When the resurgence of football in America petered out, he returned to these shores to become the Welsh National Team Manager. Despite having some outstanding players in Rush, Ratcliffe and Southall, Wales still fell some way short of qualifying for the major competitions and this prompted the Welsh F.A. to sack him in 1988.

WALLY & HOWARD TALBOT PHOTOGRAPHY

DEREK FAZACKERLEY

Birthplace:	Preston
Born:	5th November 1951
Position:	Centre-Back

Football League Career

	Appearances	Goals
Blackburn Rovers	593 (3)	24
Chester City	66	0
Total	659 (3)	24

Born in Preston on 5th November 1951, Derek Fazackerley joined Blackburn Rovers virtually straight from school. He graduated to the first team in 1971, his breakthrough coninciding with one of the bleakest periods in the club's history. But through it all, 'Faz', as he was fondly known to all Rovers supporters, remained unperturbed at the centre of the defence, turning in his usually reliable performances week after week.

Dominant in the air and a strong tackler, he was the cornerstone of the Blackburn defence, with his greatest asset being his consistency. It was a tribute to his performances that on the rare occasions he had a bad match, it was noticed immediately as being totally out of character. He was also extremely quick over the ground, his pace enabling him to recover lost ground with ease.

He was always at his best when playing alongside a traditional centre-half, almost as a sweeper. His game flourished when he was partnered with Glenn Keeley, an arrangement that Howard Kendall, when he took over as manager, gave his full encouragement.

'Faz' didn't score too many League goals, 24 in all, but his best will certainly linger in the author's mind as well as many Rovers supporters'. As a Bolton fan, I was standing on the Embankment at Burnden Park when he scored the only goal of a tension-charged local derby on 28th March 1973. I suppose there are few outside of Blackburn who will recognise the name or recall the player, for Fazackerley wasn't honoured at international level. Derek Fazackerley was 'Mr Consistency' to many Ewood supporters and when he passed Ronnie Clayton's all-time appearance record for Blakcburn Rovers, he wrote a new page in the history of the club.

In 1979, Oldham Athletic offered £60,000 for his services, but fortunately for Rovers he opted to stay at Ewood. In 1987, when he seemed to be at the end of his playing career, he was allowed to join Chester City as player-assistant manager. A year later, he joined former Rovers boss Bob Saxton at York City, before in February 1989 he teamed up with his old friend Martin Dobson at Bury.

He left the League scene in the summer of 1989 after having played a total of 662 League games (including appearances as substitute) before in May of last year, he was appointed player-manager of Finnish club Kumu.

LANCASHIRE EVENING TELEGRAPH

TOM FINNEY

Birthplace:	Preston
Born:	5th April 1922
Position:	Winger; Centre-Forward

Football League Career

	Appearances	Goals
Preston North End	433	187
Total	433	187
England International Appearances		76
Goals		30

Tom Finney graced the footballing scene in all parts of the world for many a long day, though he spent his entire League career with his home-town club, Preston North End. He resisted all temptations to move into more fashionable clubs and because of this loyalty, he failed to win any major domestic honours.

He was registered by North End as an amateur in the Preston and District League in 1937 at the age of 15. In 1939 he made his debut at outside-right for North End juniors against Manchester United juniors. On 25th January 1940, he was registered as a professional.

He won war-time honours in the shape of a Cup winners' medal and Second Division Championship medal. The Football League War Cup Final with Arsenal was drawn at Wembley, North End winning the replay at Blackburn. Finney was still a youngster trying to make his name, but he turned the England captain, Eddie Hapgood, inside out. In July 1945, he gained his first representative honours for the F.A. XI in Zurich.

He made his Football League debut in the opening game of the first season after World War Two against Leeds United, when he scored the first of 187 League goals.

A versatile player, he was able to play with equal ease on the right or left flank and even at centre-forward.

On 28th September 1946, he made his international debut for England against Ireland in Belfast, scoring the first of thirty goals. He made 76 England appearances, 40 at outside-right, 33 at outside-left and three at centre-forward, his 30 goals for England equalling the record that was shared by Nat Lofthouse at the time. In his 76 games, he was on the losing side a mere twelve occasions. He hit a hat-trick against Portugal in Lisbon in 1950, as England won 5-3. He began his England career at outside-right, the berth in which Stan Matthews won world-wide renown. Soon, however, Matthews was back and Tom did more than settle contentedly for the role of outside-left. He gave a devastating display in a 10-0 win against Portugal and then for years figured with Matthews in one of the greatest wing combinations the world has ever seen. For years the fans and critics compared his merits with those of his great contemporary, Stanley Matthews. When people were unwise enough to ask a man of such modesty if he was better than his close friend, Finney would reply with sincerity, "To me Stanley Matthews is phenomenal."

In 1954, Finney appeared in the F.A. Cup Final at Wembley, but West Bromwich Albion won 3-2, depriving him of a major honour. However, he was elected Footballer of the Year that season and again in 1957, the first man to win it twice.

In 1957-58, playing at centre-forward, he scored 26 goals to help Preston to the First Division runners-up spot behind Wolves. Finney destroyed defences and was one of soccer's keenest competitors ever, yet never received a booking or even a hard word from a referee.

Liverpool manager Bill Shankly's only criticism of Finney was that he didn't play for Liverpool! Reckoning that he was the best attacking player he'd ever seen, he wrote that, "If I were pressed into it, I would say that Tom was the best player ever born."

He retired in 1960 at the age of 38, having devoted his entire career to North End and England. In 1963, he 'guested' in his only European club game for the Irish team Distiillery in their Cup tie against Benfica.

Known as the 'Preston Plumber' because he continued to run his plumbing business during his playing days, he was awarded the O.B.E. for his services to the game.

WALLY & HOWARD TALBOT PHOTOGRAPHY

BILL FOULKES

Birthplace:	St Helens
Born:	5th January 1932
Position:	Full-Back; Centre-Half

Football League Career

	Appearances	Goals
Manchester United	563 (3)	7
Total	563 (3)	7

England International Appearances	1
Goals	0

Born in St Helens, Bill Foulkes joined Manchester United as a lad from Whiston Boys' Club in 1949, turning professional in August 1951 for a £10 signing-on fee. He used to work at the pit face, but the Red Devils brought him into first-class football in 1952, when he made his League debut at full-back in a 2-1 win at Anfield.

In those days, he was rather raw and an ungainly full-back. It was in this position that he won his one and only international cap, playing for England against Northern Ireland in 1954. The following season, he played in two England Under-23 matches and for the Football League – that was the extent of his representative football.

Bill Foulkes was a strong and most reliable defender and he gave Manchester United sterling service during his 18 years in the first team. In 1958, he had been a member of the United squad which was decimated at Munich after the Reds had defeated Red Star Belgrade in the European Cup over the two legs. Foulkes survived Munich to become the backbone of United's defence around which Matt Busby began to rebuild. He and Harry Gregg were the only two survivors who played in the first game after the disaster – the 3-0 F.A. Cup win over Sheffield Wednesday. Foulkes' successful conversion to centre-half led to him holding the number five spot for over ten years. United got to the F.A. Cup Final that year, only to lose to Bolton. Foulkes was the captain. He gained compensation for his two losers' medals (he was also there in 1957) when United beat Leicester City 3-1 in 1963.

His rugged courage and first-time tackling served United well. Not a great goalscorer – though he notched four League goals in 1966-67 – it was perhaps fitting that Bill Foulkes should score in United's 3-3 draw with Real Madrid which put the Reds into the 1968 European Cup Final.

It was obvious that he couldn't go on forever, though even towards the end of his 21-year association with the Reds, he showed little or no diminution in either skill or dominance, though a little of his speed had vanished and he wasn't quite so quick on the turn.

He played the last of his 682 first-team games for United against Southampton at the start of the 1969-70 season. He had won four League Championship medals, played in three F.A. Cup Finals and had been a member of United's

1968 European Cup winning team. On his retirement, he was appointed youth team coach and a year later was promoted to reserve team coach. He then went to America to manage Chicago Stings, switching to Tulsa Roughnecks shortly after. During the early 1980s, he was manager-coach of the Norwegian side, Lillestrom, and in 1989, he managed the Japanese side Mazda.

MANCHESTER EVENING NEWS

SIMON GARNER

Birthplace: Boston
Born: 23rd November 1959
Position: Forward

Football League Career

	Appearances	Goals
Blackburn Rovers	441 (18)	163
Total	441 (18)	163

Arriving at Ewood Park as a schoolboy in the summer of 1976, Simon Garner impressed both the Youth and Central League sides, before making his first-team debut at the age of 18 in a League Cup match at Exeter. A few days later, he made his League debut when he appeared as a substitute at Newcastle.

Originally, he was used in midfield, but during the promotion campaign of 1979-80, manager Howard Kendall successfully converted him to inside-forward, where he formed a great partnership with Andy Kennedy for the last third of that season. It was during Kendall's reign as manager, that Garner almost joined Halifax Town for a fee somewhere in the region of £40,000, but fortunately for Rovers, he was reluctant to move.

When Bob Saxton replaced Kendall as manager, Garner seemed to find a new lease of life, his pace and power making him a handful for the Second Division defences. He capitalised on many defensive errors, notably the mistimed back-passes that many defenders rued.

In 1982-83, he scored 22 League goals – it was his best season. On 10th September 1983, Simon Garner scored all five goals, including a penalty as Rovers beat Derby County 5-1 in a Second Division match at Ewood Park. He hit another hat-trick towards the end of that season as Blackburn beat Portsmouth 4-2 at Fratton Park.

During the 1980s, Garner won recognition as one of the deadliest marksmen outside of the First Division.

At the start of the 1986-87 season, he hit four goals as Blackburn beat Sunderland 6-1. Another hat-trick followed on 3rd September 1988 as Rovers beat Lancashire neighbours Oldham 3-1.

He established a goalscoring record for Blackburn Rovers that season. He took his aggregate total to 144 goals to overhaul the record set by Tommy Briggs of 140 League goals between 1952 and 1958. The record came in the match against Manchester City. If he scored more than one goal, he would create history, having scored more League goals than any other player in the club's history. He scored in the 13th minute and almost broke the record early in the second half after having a shot cleared off the line, after nutmegging the City 'keeper. After 74 minutes, the record was broken; moving to the left of the penalty area, he hit a beautiful cross shot into the far side of the net. For good measure, three minutes later, he completed his hat-trick, Rovers winning 4-0. Garner finished the season with 20 goals, his second best total.

It has remained a mystery (he hit another hat-trick against Barnsley in September 1989) why no First Division club came in for him. Blackburn have in recent years come close to promotion, though Simon Garner has remained loyal to the one club (gaining a deserved testimonial in 1988) where his goalscoring exploits have proved so valuable.

LANCASHIRE EVENING TELEGRAPH

ANDY GRAY

Birthplace:	Glasgow
Born:	30th November 1955
Position:	Forward

Football League Career

	Appearances	Goals
Aston Villa	165 (2)	59
Wolverhampton Wanderers	130 (3)	38
Everton	44 (5)	14
Notts County	3 (1)	0
West Bromwich Albion	30 (2)	10
Total	372 (13)	121

Scotland International Appearances	20
Goals	7

Moving to Villa Park from Dundee United in 1975, Andy Gray had been around for some years when he signed for Everton.

As an Aston Villa star, he had become the first man in the history of the game to receive both the Player of the Year and the Young Player of the Year awards in the same season from the Professional Footballers' Association.

He moved to Wolves for a British record fee of £1,469,000 and made his debut at Goodison, scoring in their 3-2 victory. His career was going nowhere at Molineux and Everton manager Howard Kendall was able to secure his services for just £250,000 in November 1983.

Gray was prone to injury and many considered him too old when he arrived at Everton. It took some weeks for Gray to make his presence felt at Goodison, but he went on to display a new zest for the game, proving to be an important and exciting capture. A very special relationship was forged between Andy Gray and the Everton fans, as he became one of the inspirational figures behind the Blues' great eighties revival.

During that 1983-84 season, he was cup-tied and unavailable for action in the Milk Cup, but was very much involved in the F.A. Cup. In the sixth round at Meadow Lane, he scored a remarkable winner to defeat Notts County. Launching himself along the slippery ground, he made contact with the ball only inches from the surface to send a superb diving header inside Mick Leanard's right-hand post.

In the final against Watford, he scored one of the goals in Everton's 2-0 triumph. Many people thought he fouled goalkeeper Sherwood when he jumped for the ball in front of the posts, but as the video shows, Gray never touched him!

After playing his part in the League Championship success of 1985 and the European Cup Winners' Cup victory over Rapid Vienna in Rotterdam, he was allowed to return to Aston Villa, as the Blues signed Gary Lineker. The Goodison faithful sent petitions to manager Kendall to record their great disappointment at his departure.

A Scottish international with 20 caps, he had certainly left his mark on Everton Football Club, following in the footsteps of Dean, Lawton, Royle and Latchford.

His stay at Goodison was comparatively short, just 20 months, yet he scored some crucial goals and inspired all those around him.

LIVERPOOL DAILY POST & ECHO

HARRY GREGG

Birthplace:	Magherafelt, Nr Derry
Born:	25th October 1932
Position:	Goalkeeper

Football League Career

	Appearances	Goals
Doncaster Rovers	93	0
Manchester United	211	0
Stoke City	2	0
Total	306	0

Northern Ireland International Appearances	25
Goals	0

Harry Gregg began his footballing career with Dundalk and was a part-timer with Coleraine and Linfield, earning £11 per week as a joiner, before he was snapped up by Doncaster Rovers in the summer of 1951. He turned professional at Belle Vue on his 20th birthday in October 1952. Matt Busby signed him for Manchester United in December 1957 for what was then a record for a goalkeeper – £23,000. Gregg made his debut almost immediately in the match against Leicester City.

The New Year began well for Gregg and Manchester United. A 3-2 home win over Red Star Belgrade in the European Cup was followed by a 3-3 draw in Belgrade. The Irishman was in superb form, saving shot after shot that by rights should have seen United out of the competition. However, his form was such that United won a place in the European Cup semi-finals. The day after United's thrilling 3-3 draw in Belgrade, tragedy struck. The plane that was carrying home the victorious United team crashed on the runway at Munich Airport, killing many of the players. Harry Gregg crawled virtually unscathed from the wreckage and as the plane's crew shouted for people to get away from the aircraft for fear of fire, he returned to the plane and helped some of the passengers to safety, including a 22-month-old baby girl. Remarkably, three weeks later, Gregg played in the 3-0 win over Sheffield Wednesday in the F.A. Cup and three months later in the Final at Wembley against Bolton Wanderers. He had a great contest with Bolton and England centre-forward Nat Lofthouse, but there was to be no fairy tale ending as Bolton ran out winners 2-0. Gregg was the victim of the controversial challenge made by Lofthouse, who bundled both Gregg and the ball over the line. Today, Nat admits he would be sent off!

Despite his disappointments at Wembley, Gregg had a superb year at international level, as Northern Ireland qualified for the World Cup Finals. The bulk of the Irish party flew to Sweden, but Gregg, with the Munich disaster fresh in his mind, sailed separately by ferry.

In the last group match, Ireland needed at least one point from their match against West Germany, the reigning world champions. Surprisingly, with about ten minutes

MANCHESTER EVENING NEWS

left, the Irish led 2-1, though Gregg was injured and playing virtually on one leg. He was diving all over the penalty area, though a late equaliser from Uwe Seeler meant that Ireland had to play Czechoslovakia in a play-off match. Gregg wasn't fit, but Ireland qualified. Unfortunately, the injury-hit Irish were beaten 4-0 by France in the quarter-final. Harry Gregg was acclaimed by the viewing public as the best 'keeper in those finals.

Gregg was tall, slim and very well-built and continued his superb displays for the Reds and for Northern Ireland until December 1966, when he signed on a permanent basis for Stoke city after a loan period at the Victoria Ground. In 1967, he retired from the game as a player to take over at Shrewsbury as manager. He also managed Swansea and Crewe before in 1982-83 he returned to Vetch Field as coach after a stint abroad with the Kitan Sports Club in Kuwait. In July 1984, he was appointed assistant to Lou Macari at Swindon Town but departed in April 1985 after the two former United stars ended up not speaking to each other!

BRUCE GROBBELAAR

Birthplace: Durban, South Africa
Born: 6th October 1957
Position: Goalkeeper

Football League Career

	Appearances	Goals
Crewe Alexandra	24	1
Liverpool	369	0
Total	393	1

Perhaps there was no-one more aptly named than Bruce Grobbelaar, for translated from the original Dutch, his surname means 'clumsy'. Though born in Durban, he moved to Rhodesia (now Zimbabwe) with his family. Soon, he was a schoolboy professional, playing for an all-white team, the Salisbury Callies, in a multi-racial league. At 16, he made his international debut for Rhodesia, but after a row with the club manager, he walked out and joined the Rhodesian Army. At the time, Rhodesia was in the grip of a civil war and the army was fighting the bush guerillas. After two years, he returned to civilian life and started to play for Durban City in South Africa. A trial was arranged with West Bromwich Albion, but after four months, he moved to Fourth Division Bournemouth.

Disappointed, he signed for Canadian club, Vancouver Whitecaps. After a season, mostly as substitute, he was loaned to Crewe Alexandra, who were 92nd in the Football League. He played 24 games for Crewe, it soon becoming apparent that he was a fun-loving character and in one game for Alex, he scored from the penalty spot!

He had another spell with the Whitecaps before in March 1981, he joined Liverpool in a surprise transfer deal of £250,000, Bob Paisley obviously recognising his great natural ability.

The Kop loved his stunning saves, his sharp reflexes and the way he dominated his penalty area. In his first three seasons with the club, he was an ever-present and won three League Championship winners' medals. They were followed by the F.A. Cup and Milk Cup. In 1984, Liverpool won their fourth European Cup, beating A.S. Roma in a penalty shoot-out, during which Bruce even found time to perform a 'knobbly-knees' routine, much to the delight of the Liverpool fans! But the following year's European Cup Final was overshadowed by the Heysel Stadium tragedy, at which point, Grobbelaar considered giving up football.

Probably the highlight of his career to date was the 1985-86 Double Season when he was once again an ever-present. After a bout of meningitis in 1988-89, he won his place back from Mike Hooper, as the side went 22 games undefeated.

He went through the similar heart-searching he'd gone through after Heysel, after the Hillsborough disaster of 1989. At the subsequent inquiry into the semi-final tragedy, it was revealed that Grobbelaar saved many lives by insisting that the police let fans onto the pitch before more fans were killed in the crush behind his goal. His decision to continue playing again was rewarded when Liverpool beat Everton 3-2 in the 1989 F.A. Cup Final.

He has now made over 500 appearances for Liverpool – a great goalkeeper and one of the game's biggest entertainers.

LIVERPOOL DAILY POST & ECHO

ALAN HANSEN

Birthplace: Alloa
Born: 13th June 1955
Position: Defender

Football League Career

	Appearances	Goals
Liverpool	435 (2)	7
Total	435 (2)	7

Scotland International Appearances	26
Goals	0

A multi-talented sportsman as a youngster, he was also an above-average scholar, leaving Lornshill Academy with 7 'O' levels and 4 'A' levels. He had represented Scotland at golf, squash and volleyball, but it was at football that he excelled. He'd actually had a trial with Liverpool when he was 15, but had been turned down. However, when he was 21 the Reds changed their minds and Bob Paisley paid Partick Thistle £100,000 for him in April 1977.

By this time, he had played 100 games for the Scottish League side. Alan Hansen was arguably Bob Paisley's best-ever signing. He was an inspired long-term investment, as was evident when he made his debut against Derby County in a 1-0 victory on September 24th 1977, replacing the injured Phil Thompson.

The Anfield crowd were used to the uncompromising play of Ron Yeats and Tommy Smith, but Hansen's ability on the ball marked him out as a player of the highest class. His runs forward from defence as he accelerated past people as smoothly as a Roll's Royce gave Liverpool's attacks an extra dimension.

As an orthodox centre-half, he has had few peers; his excellent reading of the game was supported by firm tackling and more-than-adequate ability in the air.

Making his international debut in 1979 and playing in the 1982 World Cup tournament, his failure to win more than 26 Socttish caps was a great mystery. He was even omitted from the 1986 World Cup party by Alex Ferguson. His constant rejection by his country's national team selectors may well go down as one of the great blunders in Scottish football. He most surely would have been a permanent fixture in any other national side of the modern era.

He replaced Phil Neal as captain in October 1985; it was his leadership that played a vital part in the Reds' League and Cup double that season. It was probably his greatest moment in his illustrious career, for he became one of only five captains in the history of the game to lift the League Championship trophy and the F.A. Cup in the same season. Whoever he has partnered in the centre of the Reds' defence – Thompson, Lawrenson, Gillespie and Hysen – he has thrived. The most flourishing was the superb partnership he formed with Eire international

Mark Lawrenson until the latter was forced to retire in 1987.

Hansen possessed the ability to make time and space to use the ball effectively. He set up John Aldridge's goal against Manchester United in November 1987, with a beautifully chipped pass to Steve McMahon who put the Eire international in.

It was realised during the 1988-89 season, when he had a lengthy lay-off, that the knee trouble he had suffered throughout his career was going to limit his appearances. So it came as no surprise to learn during last season that he was retiring from the game, but it was rather startling that he didn't anticipate staying in the game in some other capacity.

Hansen played in 608 first-team games for Liverpool, a record of consistency and quality that have established him as one of the most outstanding post-war defenders and set him alongside the greatest names in Liverpool's glittering modern history.

LIVERPOOL DAILY POST & ECHO

ASA HARTFORD

Birthplace: Clydebank
Born: 24th October 1950
Position: Midfield

Football League Career

	Appearances	Goals
West Bromwich Albion	206 (8)	18
Manchester City	259 (1)	29
Notts Forest	3	0
Everton	81	6
Norwich City	28	2
Bolton Wanderes	83	8
Stockport County	30 (1)	0
Total	690 (10)	63

Scotland International Appearances	50
Goals	4

Born in Clydebank, Asa Hartford was named after the celebrated American singer Al (Asa) Jolson.

He was plucked from Scottish amateur football after being spotted by a West Bromwich Albion scout and signed professional forms for them in 1967, playing for them in the League Cup Final some three years later. He was soon thrilling the crowds with his mature skill and vision and it was only a matter of time before the inevitable big-money offer arrived to tempt Albion. Hartford will probably always be remembered as the player whose transfer to then First Division giants Leeds United was sensationally called off after a routine medical examination revealed a hole-in-the-heart condition. That was almost twenty years ago, in 1972, when he was poised to move from the Hawthorns to Elland Road for £170,000.

Showing great durability, the condition, happily for Asa, was a minor one and in August 1974, he joined Manchester City for £225,000. Making his debut against West Ham United, he swept away all doubts about his fitness with his stamina and urgent play in midfield. He went on to play a major role in City's glorious era of the late 1970s, picking up a League-Cup winners' medal with them in 1976.

In June 1979, he signed for Notts Forest under the management of Brian Clough for £500,000, but after only 63 days and three League games, he was on his way back to the north-west and Everton.

He had already clocked up transfer fees worth a small fortune, before his £400,000 move to Goodison.

Hartford was a wily character, quick of temper and determined, but also gifted and the kind of midfield terrier every successful team needs. After two seasons and 98 appearances for Everton, he moved back to Manchester City for £350,000 and a second spell. When City bought him for the second time, he was still a current Scottish international player. He won 50 Scottish caps, 35 of them in his two spells with Manchester City.

He played in 317 first-team games for City in his two spells before in May 1984, he said farewell to Maine Road and had a spell in the North American Soccer League with Fort Lauderdale Sun.

He later returned to First Division action with Norwich City. He helped the Canaries win the 1985 Milk Cup when his shot was deflected by Sunderland's Chisholm for the only goal of the game.

In July 1985, he was granted a free-transfer and joined Bolton Wanderers. He was a great inspiration at Burnden Park, becoming club captain and an ever-present during 1985-86. He was at Wembley again in May 1986 as Bolton lost 3-0 to Bristol City in the Freight Rover Final. Unfortunately, despite Asa's great experience, the Trotters were relegated to the Fourth Division for the first time in their history, though they bounced back straight away.

He went on to join Stockport County as player-manager on a free-transfer, before joining Shrewsbury as manager. In January 1991 he was relieved of his post at Gay Meadow and returned to Lancashire, playing a few games for Bury reserves.

His first-class soccer career had spanned two decades and seen 700 League appearances.

MANCHESTER EVENING NEWS

COLIN HARVEY

Birthplace:	Liverpool
Born:	16th November 1944
Position:	Midfield

Football League Career

	Appearances	Goals
Everton	317 (3)	18
Sheffield Wednesday	45	2
Total	362 (3)	20

England International Appearances	1
Goals	0

Brought up in Fazackerley in the north end of Liverpool, Colin Harvey attended the Holy Name School, where he showed his potential as the side won both the Cup and League competitions. 'Transferred' to the Cardinal Allen High School, he was relieved that the boys who had come through the 13-plus examination were allowed to play soccer, for it was a rugby stronghold.

As a youngster, he had a trial with Liverpool and was told to come back the following week, but in the meantime, he was invited for a trial at Goodison. Offered professional terms, he jumped at the chance, thoroughly enjoying the discipline and training that were part of a football apprentice's life.

With Jimmy Gabriel injured, Everton manager Harry Catterick was forced to give a debut to the home-grown 18-year-old Harvey in the Second Leg of the First Round of the European Cup against Inter Milan in the San Siro Stadium. The first leg at Goodison had been goalless and though Harvey played with a maturity and experience, Everton lost by the only goal of the game.

After that baptism of fire, he managed just two First Division games that season, but established himself in the side in 1964-65, after playing in a tough encounter with Manchester United in mid-September. Two days later, he played in his first Merseyside derby; Everton beating their arch-rivals 4-0 with Harvey getting on the scoresheet. He played in 32 games that season, as the Blues ended the campaign in fourth place.

I was at Burnden Park in 1966 when Everton played champions Manchester United in the semi-final of the F.A. Cup. The Blues soaked up the United pressure and then counter-attacked with Colin Harvey shooting them into the Final, where they beat Sheffield Wednesday 3-2.

Colin Harvey's finest quality was his vision and his ability to spray long accurate passes to his forwards, while at the same time he would effectively block any impending attacks by the opposition through his brilliant positional play.

He only won one England cap; that was in 1971 when Malta were beaten 1-0.

Harvey was the stabilising influence in the magnificent midfield trio that was instrumental in Everton winning

LIVERPOOL DAILY POST & ECHO

the 1970 Championship. Though slightly built, he won the ball in tackles with the great timing of his challenges. He gave everything in a match, he didn't know how to play it any other way – he was the sort of player that all managers would love to have in their team.

After playing in more than 380 first-team games for the Blues he moved to Sheffield Wednesday for £70,000 in 1974. A nagging hip injury caught up with him late in his career and he had to retire in 1976. He resumed his links with Everton through the coaching ranks where, despite having a hip replacement, he took a full active role in the training programme. In 1987, he was the people's choice to succeed Howard Kendall as manager. A single-minded individual, he lost his position when Kendall returned in 1990, but within a couple of days, the two were together again.

STEVE HEIGHWAY

Birthplace:	Dublin
Born:	25th November 1947
Position:	Winger

Football League Career

	Appearances	Goals
Liverpool	312 (17)	50
Total	312 (17)	50

Republic of Ireland International Appearances	34
Goals	0

Steve Heighway did not see a football match until he was ten years old, but he took to the game straight away after that. He was with Manchester City when he was 17 and although they gave him every opportunity to enjoy a footballer's life, his education always came first. He had done well at school – well enough that he eventually won a place at Warwick University.

Even at 21, when most footballers have five years of their full-time careers behind them, Steve wasn't contemplating turning professional, never mind becoming part of one of the world's most successful teams. Fortunately, soccer has a good scouting system and if you're any good they'll catch you at any age.

Steve was playing for Skelmersdale United, the Lancashire club that was earning a growing reputation in the old Amateur Cup, when he was caught, and within weeks he was in the Liverpool first team.

Though he and his family are English, he was born in Dublin and was chosen for Eire before he'd played in the Liverpool first team, against Poland in Dublin in September 1970. Eire lost 2-0.

Heighway bought pace and width to the Liverpool attack, having a two-footed talent which enabled him to cut inside opponents or go past them on the outside. In the months following his first-team debut, he turned the tide in the Merseyside derby, with Liverpool two down. He scored the first from an acute angle and then provided the cross for John Toshack to equalise before Chris Lawler hit the winner. He ended his first campaign with a near post shot that deceived Arsenal 'keeper Bob Wilson to give Liverpool the lead in the 1971 F.A. Cup Final but the Gunners hit back to win.

By the mid 1970s, he had become one of Liverpool's most consistent performers, spending much of his time in deep lying positions and prompting the success of the Keegan-Toshack partnership.

Despite wearing the number nine shirt, Heighway was a winger with the audacity to take on defenders and confound them. He ran at the defenders and went past them time and time again. Occasionally, he over-elaborated, but his ability to cross the ball at full speed gave the Reds a new dimension to their attacking play. His cross for McDermott to head home in such style against Spurs in September

LIVERPOOL DAILY POST & ECHO

1978 was a prime example.
His main task with Liverpool had been to penetrate on the flanks, but he was a constant factor in a forward line that often opted to do without an orthodox centre-forward. At the end of the decade, he crossed the Atlantic to end his playing days with Minnesota Kicks. He later returned to Anfield to coach the youngsters. An Anfield to coach the youngsters. Bill Shankly once said,"Heighway is an individualist. He can win a match with one flash of genius."

DAVID HERD

Birthplace: Hamilton
Born: 15th April 1934
Position: Inside-Forward; Centre-Forward

Football League Career

	Appearances	Goals
Stockport County	16	6
Arsenal	166	97
Manchester United	201 (1)	114
Stoke City	39 (5)	11
Total	422 (6)	228

Scotland International Appearances	5
Goals	4

David Herd is the son of the former Manchester City and Stockport County inside-forward Alec Herd. He began his career at Edgeley Park in 1949 and turned professional in 1951. Alec Herd had won F.A. Cup and Championship medals with Manchester City, a feat that son David was to emulate with Manchester United. In fact, when David Herd turned out at inside-left for Stockport County in the final game of the 1950-51 Third Division North campaign and his father Alec played inside-right, it was only the second time that father and son had played in the same League team.

After five years and only 16 appearances for Stockport, he moved to Arsenal in 1954 for £8,000. Herd could play at either centre-or inside-forward and packed a powerful shot. He won five Scottish cups with the Gunners, although he wore the number seven shirt in one of them. He signed for United for a fee of £35,000 in the summer of 1961, after finishing second to Jimmy Greaves in the First Division goalscoring charts the previous season. He had played in over 200 competitive games for Arsenal and scored 125 goals.

He made his debut for the Reds in London on the opening day of the 1961-62 season as United drew 1-1 with West Ham and ended the season as top scorer for the club. His two goals in the 1963 F.A. Cup Final repaid a large slice of his transfer fee as United beat Leicester City 3-1. He scored the first of his five hat-tricks for United on 14th December 1963 as they beat Sheffield Wednesday 3-1 at Old Trafford.

In November 1966, Herd scored a very unusual hat-trick for United against Sunderland at Old Trafford. He struck three goals past three different goalkeepers – Jim Montgomery who went off injured, his replacement Charlie Hurley, and his deputy John Parke. He added a fourth in United's 5-0 win. His fifth and final hat-trick came the following month as United won a seven goal thriller 4-3 against West Brom at the Hawthorns.

A key member of the 1965 and 1967 Championship teams, his best season in finding the net was 1965-66 when he scored 32 goals in his 50 appearances in all competitions (24 in the League from 36 appearances). He only made a handful of appearances in United's European Cup winning season and after 263 first-team games and 144 goals, he moved to Stock City in July 1968.

He wound down his League career with the Potters before signing for Ireland club Waterford in December 1970. Three months later, he became manager of Lincoln City, where he remained for 21 months. Still a good cricketer, David is opening batsman for Cheadle Hulme, one of Cheshire's top club sides.

MANCHESTER EVENING NEWS

DAVE HICKSON

Birthplace:	Salford
Born:	30th October 1929
Position:	Centre-Forward

Football League Career

	Appearances	Goals
Everton	255	95
Aston Villa	12	1
Huddersfield Town	54	28
Liverpool	60	37
Bury	8	0
Tranmere Rovers	45	21
Total	404	182

Born in Salford, Dave Hickson had a leaning to Manchester United as a boy, but his family moved to Ellesmere Port, where Dave made a great impression at Schoolboy level. Everton scout Tom Corley spotted him playing for Ellesmere Port Town and invited him to attend trials. He finally signed professional forms for Everton in 1948, but almost immediately, his career had to be put on 'hold' as he was called up by the Army. He eventually made his League debut in 1951-52, the Blues' first season in the Second Division. He played in 31 League games and scored a creditable 14 goals.

In the 5th Round of the 1952-53 F.A. Cup, Everton entertained Manchester United at Goodison. By the end of the match, the name of Dave Hickson was on everybody's lips. Just before half-time and with the score standing at 1-1, he was led off the field with a badly cut eyebrow. He returned for the second period with blood still streaming down his face and though the referee twice suggested he should go off, he refused. After 64 minutes, he picked up the ball just outside the United box, beat one man, side-stepped another and hit his shot into the back of the net for the winning goal. Hickson also scored the only goal of the 6th Round as Everton won at Villa Park. Receiving the ball out on the right-hand touchline and just inside his own half, he played the ball to Buckle in the outside left position, before racing to take the return pass and ram the ball home. Everton lost 4-3 to Bolton Wanderers in the semi-final, again showing great fighting spirit as they'd been 4-0 down at half-time.

The Everton crowd loved Dave Hickson, but his robust style often got him into trouble with the officials – he was sent off three times in his career, but only once for a bad tackle.

In November 1955, Everton sold him to Aston Villa for £20,000. He then moved to Huddersfield Town, but in July 1957 he returned to Goodison for £6,500 – he'd only been away 18 months and Everton had made a handsome profit on his transfer.

During the 1959-60 season, he was dropped three times and so arch-rivals Liverpool, who'd just lost Billy Liddell through injury, put in a bid for him. There was uproar in the city from both sets of supporters, but on 7th November 1959, Hickson signed for Liverpool for £12,000. Some Everton fans swore they would follow him to Anfield, whilst a contingent of Liverpool's Koppites pledged to make the opposite journey. He had scored 111 goals in 243 first-team appearances for Everton.

He made his Liverpool debut against one of his former clubs, Aston Villa; Hickson scoring both goals in a 2-1 win. He transformed the Reds' season, scoring 21 goals in 27 games.

A quiet man off the pitch, he was a constant victim of provocation on it. Playing for Liverpool against Sheffield United, he was sent off for retaliation, but was later cleared of deliberate violent conduct. Known as 'The Cannonball Kid', he had been coached by the legendary Dixie Dean and was instrumental in the early development of Roger Hunt. He scored 38 goals in his 67 appearances for the Reds before moving on to Bury and finally Tranmere Rovers, thus playing for all three Merseyside League clubs.

LIVERPOOL DAILY POST & ECHO

FREDDIE HILL

Birthplace:	Sheffield
Born:	17th January 1940
Position:	Inside-Forward

Football League Career

	Appearances	Goals
Bolton Wanderers	373 (2)	74
Halifax Town	25	3
Manchester City	28 (7)	3
Peterborough United	73 (2)	7
Total	499 (11)	87

England International Appearances	2
Goals	0

Emerging from junior football in his home city of Sheffield, Freddie Hill signed for Bolton Wanderers in 1957. He had turned down an offer from Sheffield Wednesday in the hope of getting regular first-team football with the Lancashire club.

He made his League debut for the Wanderers in April 1958 at the age of 18, as a replacement for Dennis Stevens, in a 1-1 draw against Newcastle United at Burnden Park.

When Nat Lofthouse had to retire due to injury, it was Dennis Stevens who replaced him at centre-forward, allowing Freddie Hill to become a permanent member of the attack at inside-forward. He had already begun to show his goalscoring ability when he netted 7 goals from his 18 appearances in 1958-59.

On 4th March 1959, he hit the first of two hat-tricks for the Wanderers in a 6-0 mauling of Chelsea on a very windy night. In the 1961-62 campaign, he netted 14 goals in 41 games – it was his best return to date.

After only three seasons in League football, his ability was recognised when he was selected for the England Under-23 side. In October 1962, he was chosen to play in his first full international against Northern Ireland in Belfast. In November of the same year, he played against Wales at Wembley, but it was his last appearance in an England shirt. The third-round F.A. Cup tie against Sheffield United at Bramall Lane was played at the 13th attempt, but Wanderers lost 3-1. There was an immediate revenge however, for Freddie Hill hit his second hat-trick to secure the points against United in Bolton's first home League game for three months.

In the two-year period 1962-64, Freddie Hill asked for a move on four occasions. His last request was accepted with great regret, for Hill was a firm favourite with the Burnden fans. Liverpool were set to pay £60,000 for him, but withdrew their offer after Hill failed a medical, due to high blood pressure.

The 1964-65 season was Hill's best in terms of goals, the scheming inside-forward hitting 15 goals in 41 matches. He played until the end of the 1968-69 campaign, playing

in 412 games for the Whites and scoring 79 goals.
He left Bolton in July 1969 in a £5,000 deal, for Halifax Town, but within a year, he was back in the top flight with Manchester City who paid the Yorkshire side £12,000 for Hill's services. At Maine Road, he teamed up with Francis Lee and Wyn Davies to revive old Bolton partnerships.
In August 1973, he moved to Peterborough United, where he ended his League career. He returned to the north-west, playing for both Droylsden and Radcliffe Borough.
In October 1990, this popular player was granted a late but thoroughly deserved testimonial when Bolton Wanderers entertained Manchester City.

MANCHESTER EVENING NEWS

DOUG HOLDEN

Birthplace:	Manchester
Born:	28th September 1930
Position:	Winger

Football League Career

	Appearances	Goals
Bolton Wanderers	419	40
Preston North End	89	13
Total	508	53

England International Appearances	5
Goals	0

Doug Holden began his footballing career in his native Manchester with Princess Road School. He later joined Manchester Y.M.C.A., the Lancashire Amateur League side, for whom his three brothers all played.

Signing as an amateur for Bolton Wanderers in 1948, he appeared for England Youth before completing his National Service.

He made his League debut for the Wanderers against Liverpool in a 1-1 draw at Anfield in November 1951. He was only 17, but quickly proved that he possessed the temperament for the big occasion. He'd only made 12 appearances for the Wanderers Reserves in the Central League before his promotion to the first-team. Holden made 25 appearances that season, playing primarily on the left flank, but it was on the opposite wing that he made a name for himself, playing in the 1953 F.A. Cup Final against Blackpool in that position.

Five years later, he had reverted to the left-wing for the 1958 F.A. Cup Final against Manchester United – in fact, he and Lofthouse were the only two Bolton players to appear in both of those Finals.

In March 1959, he played for the Football League XI against the Irish League in Dublin. Impressing in that match, he was selected for the full England side against Scotland at Wembley. He only made 5 appearances for England – I just cannot understand why he didn't make more.

His best season goalscoring-wise was 1961-62, Holden hitting 11 goals from 32 appearances.

In November 1962, after spending 11 seasons with the Wanderers, he joined neighbours Preston North End.

At Preston, he proved himself a worthy addition to a lengthy list of mature, ready-made players who went to Deepdale after earning their reputations elsewhere. A fast, skilful winger, he fitted ideally into the intended role. At the small fee he cost, he was a bargain. Perhaps more than that, he showed he had far from lost his craft and know-how, with a brilliant performance in the F.A. Cup semi-final win over Swansea and a goal in the 3-2 defeat by West Ham United in the Final.

Doug Holden was one of the unluckiest of players when shooting. Often the ball somehow managed to find its way to the woodwork or else a defender miraculously got in the way.

His chief asset was his ability to work well in a confined space. Often there didn't seem room to squeeze a football between the line and the full-back, but somehow Doug got through.ball as well!

After ending his League career at Deepdale, he emigrated to Australia in 1965, becoming player-coach for Hakoah and Auburn in Sydney. He also played for the Australian national side.

In November 1970, he returned to England, having spells as trainer at Grimsby and manager of Southern League side Dartford, before leaving the game to become a car salesman.

LANCASHIRE EVENING TELEGRAPH

EDDIE HOPKINSON

Birthplace:	Wheatley Hill
Born:	29th October 1935
Position:	Goalkeeper

Football League Career

	Appearances	Goals
Oldham Athletic	3	0
Bolton Wanderers	519	0
Total	519	0

England International Appearances	14
Goals	0

Born in Wheatley Hill, County Durham, Eddie Hopkinson became a 'naturalised' Lancastrian when his family moved south to Royton, near Oldham. He was soon signed as an amateur for Oldham Athletic and was only 16 years of age when he played in three Third Division North games in 1951-52.

In the summer months, he played cricket for Royton in the Central Lancashire League and until football stopped him, he was a county water-polo player.

At the end of the 1951-52 season, Oldham Athletic overlooked him to Bolton's lasting satisfaction. He joined the Wanderers in August 1952, signing professional forms the following November. He played little football for Bolton during National Service as he was stationed in Scotland.

His meteoric rise began in August 1956 when Bolton's regular goalkeeper, Ken Grieves, the Lancashire cricketer, couldn't be released from his cricketing duties as Lancashire were chasing Championship honours. Eddie got his chance in the senior side against Blackpool and went through a brilliant first season without missing a game.

At 5ft 9 $^1/_2$ins, he was one of the smallest goalkeepers in the First Division. In the summer of 1957, he was awarded the first of six England Under-23 caps on a tour behind the Iron Curtain. In the October of that year, he made his first full international appearance against Northern Ireland, going on to play against all three countries in the Home Internationals and eventually collecting 14 caps.

In 1958, he kept a clean sheet to win an F.A. Cup winners' medal as Bolton beat Manchester United 2-0 at Wembley.

At Norwich City in January 1969, he broke Bolton's long-standing appearance record set by Alec Finney. Eddie played in 578 matches for Bolton and but for an injury which kept him out of the side for most of the 1958-59 season and another which put him out of action for a ten-match spell in the 1963-64 season, he would have passed the Finney record much earlier.

Professionals reckon that consistency is the true test of the top-class player and there were certainly few to rival Eddie Hopkinson in this aspect of his game.

He remained Bolton's first choice goalkeeper until the middle of the 1969-70 season when injury forced his retirment. He was awarded a testimonial in May 1971 at Burnden in a game which Portuguese World Cup stars Eusebio and Simoes appeared.

He became assistant trainer at Burnden Park, coaching both the Youth and Reserve sides. He left in July 1974 to join nearby Stockport County as assistant manager and where his son Paul kept goal.

He made an unexpected comeback when he volunteered to keep goal for the team he managed, Ashton United, when four players failed to show up for the Cheshire League game at Witton. Witton won 7-0, but 'Hoppy' got a great ovation as he retired at half-time to make way for latecomers.

In 1979, he returned to Bolton as goalkeeping coach, but eventually left the game to become a representative for a chemical company.

WALLY & HOWARD TALBOT PHOTOGRAPHY

EMLYN HUGHES

Birthplace:	Barrow-in-Furness
Born:	28th August 1947
Position:	Full-Back; Centre-Back; Midfield

Football League Career

	Appearances	Goals
Blackpool	27 (1)	0
Liverpool	474	35
Wolverhampton Wanderers	56 (2)	2
Rotherham United	55 (1)	6
Hull City	9	0
Swansea City	7	0
Total	628 (4)	43

England International Appearances	62
Goals	1

Born in Barrow, the son of a Welsh rugby league star, Emlyn Hughes decided that the round ball game was better suited to his talents. He began his professional career with Blackpool in September 1964, making his debut for the Seasiders in 1966 as an 18-year-old. Liverpool manager Bill Shankly was watching the game and made an offer straight after the game but had to wait ten months before signing him for £65,000 after only 27 appearances for Blackpool. 'Shanks' predicted that one day, Emlyn Hughes would lead England – and of course he was right. He was a natural for the job, his unbounding energy and infectious enthusiasm helping him to collect 62 caps. He arrived in February 1967, making his debut against Stoke City, dominating ex-Arsenal and Newcastle United international George Eastham. A few matches later, he brought down Newcastle forward Albert Bennett with a rugby tackle and was branded 'Crazy Horse' by the Kop – a nickname that he will keep forever.

He made a few appearances at left-back for the injured Gerry Byrne, but it was at left-half replacing Willie Stevenson for the 1967-68 season that he made a permanent position.

Though he played on the left side and was good with both feet, he was stronger on his right. He became known for his long-striding rampages of the First Division's grounds. His dynamic surges into the opposition's penalty box brought him a fair share of spectacular goals. One of these came against Southampton at Anfield in April 1971 when after picking up the ball just outside his own area, he played the ball wide, stormed up the centre of the park to receive the return ball before cracking home an unstoppable shot from the edge of the Saints' box.

Emlyn holds the record for the highest number of first-class matches in which any player has appeared in one season. In 1972-73, he made 74 appearances; they comprised 41 Division One games, 8 League Cup, 4 F.A. Cup, 12 U.E.F.A. Cup, 8 Internationals and an appearance in the Common Market Entry match at Wembley for

The Three v The Six.
A versatile player, in 1973-74 he moved to the centre of the Reds' defence. He also replaced Tommy Smith as captain and though perhaps he wasn't as popular as Tommy, he was a great motivator and led by example. In his five seasons as captain, he led Liverpool to 2 League Championships, 2 European Cups, 1 F.A Cup and 1 U.E.F.A. Cup.
Loved by the Anfield crowd, he was voted Footballer of the Year in 1978 and won more international caps as a Liverpool player than anyone else. After making 657 appearances in the famous Red shirt, he moved to Molineux in August 1979. It came as no surprise that he helped Wolves to League Cup success, as they beat Notts Forest 1-0 at Wembley – it was the only club trophy he needed to add to his collecton. He began to suffer with knee trouble in his stay at Wolves and moved into the lower divisions as player-manager with Rotherham United, before playing for Hull City and Swansea.
An influential figure on the field during his successful years with Liverpool and England, his personality later earned him a nationwide reputation as a television celebrity.

MANCHESTER EVENING NEWS

MARK HUGHES

Birthplace:	Wrexham	
Born:	1st November 1963	
Position:	Striker	

Football League Career

	Appearances	Goals
Manchester United	187 (8)	74
Total	187 (8)	74

Wales International Appearances	32
Goals	8

A product of Manchester United's junior system, Mark Hughes was a midfield player, later converted to centre-forward with the Reds Youth and Central League team. His first major contribution for United was in the 1981-82 F.A. Youth Cup campaign when he teamed up with Norman Whiteside to give the Reds a powerful strike force at junior level.

After making his first-team debut against Port Vale in a League Cup match, his next game was in the European Cup-Winners' Cup tie against Spartak Varna the following month. He made his League debut in March 1984, scoring a goal in United's 2-0 win over Leicester City. He made a highly encouraging start, scoring four goals in his seven full appearances that season, plus coming on in four games as substitute. He made his Welsh international debut against England in May 1984, scoring the only goal of the game. Since then, he has gone on to form a fine striking partnership with Liverpool's Ian Rush. He has scored some very spectacular goals, but the one he scored for Wales against Spain in 1985 in a World Cup qualifying game will linger long in the memory.

The following season, he was United's number one striker, scoring 25 goals in all competitions, the best individual scoring performance at Old Trafford for 13 years. He hit two hat-tricks during this campaign, against Aston Villa in the League and Burnley in the League Cup. He collected an F.A. Cup winners' medal as United beat Everton, the season ending with him being voted as the P.F.A. Young Player of the Year.

The decision to sell him to Barcelona for £2.3 million was a shock to United's supporters – many were angry and saw the sale as a betrayal. At the start of the 1985-86 campaign, United went 15 games before their first defeat – he scored 10 goals in that run as the Reds raced to the top of the table and into a commanding lead. He managed to keep a foothold in the Old Trafford camp, stating that when he did come back to England, he would only join one club, that being Manchester United.

In fact, Hughes found Spanish football difficult and in his second season, he was sent out on loan to Bayern Munich in Germany, where he was much happier.

United manager Alex Ferguson wanted to sign Hughes just before Barcelona loaned him to Bayern Munich, but

MANCHESTER EVENING NEWS

in June 1988, he clinched the deal on a player that many feel should never have been allowed to leave Old Trafford in the first place. He cost United £1.5 million, but soon began to repay some of the fee, finishing his first season back as United's leading League scorer with 14 goals, including eight in a nine-match spell.

Unquestionably brave, he was voted the P.F.A. Player of the Year in 1989, an award he picked up for a second time last season.

In 1990, it was his two goals in the 3-3 draw with Crystal Palace at Wembley that kept United in the F.A. Cup, his second coming seven minutes from the end of extra-time.

A player with a powerful, technically excellent shot, he ended last season in fine style, scoring both United's goals in the 2-1 European Cup-Winners' Cup success over Barcelona.

ROGER HUNT

Birthplace:	Golborne
Born:	20th July 1938
Position:	Forward

Football League Career

	Appearances	Goals
Liverpool	401 (3)	245
Bolton Wanderers	72 (4)	24
Total	473 (7)	269

England International Appearances	34
Goals	18

Spotted by former Liverpool and England centre-half Bill Jones, Roger Hunt had trials with Bury and Crewe before Liverpool signed him from Stockton Heath on amateur forms in 1958. He turned professional after completing his National Service and made his League debut as a 21-year-old on September 9th 1959 against Scunthorpe United at Anfield. He scored in a 2-0 victory, the first of an astonishing 285 goals in all competitions for Liverpool. He quickly secured a regular place, netting 21 goals in 36 games. In 1961-62, he helped shoot the Reds into Division One with 41 goals from 41 games, as he struck up a prolific partnership with Ian St John, thereby beating Gordon Hodgson's club record set in 1930-31.

In 1965-66, the season of their second title triumph, the Reds didn't lose a First Division game in which he scored. On September 6th 1965, he hit a hat-trick in the space of seven minutes at Upton Park as Liverpool beat West Ham 5-1. It was certainly no coincidence that Liverpool won the Championship in Hunt's two most prosperous seasons. His emergence as one of the top scorers in the country, earned him a place in Alf Ramsey's squad of 22 for the 1966 World Cup Finals. Hunt kept Jimmy Greaves out of the line-up and scored three goals, playing in all six games. It was yet another unforgettable season for Hunt – a World Cup Winners' medal, a League Championship medal and a Cup Winners' loser's medal. The Anfield fans were not slow to recognise the part Hunt played and christened him 'Sir Roger'.

There was more to Roger Hunt though than his goal scoring, which was his golden gift. He had an explosive shot and sudden and destructive pace with a phenomenal work-rate. He also possessed neat distribution, good ball control and a good footballing brain.

Roger Hunt scored some spectacular goals – a superb volley that he thrashed into the Inter Milan net during the 1965 European Cup semi-final at Anfield. An even-tempered man, Roger only once lost his temper – in March 1969, he was substituted in an F.A. Cup defeat by Leicester City and hurled his shirt into the dugout in frustration! Earlier that season, Bolton Wanderers had made moves to sign him, but Hunt, who'd supported the Burnden Park outfit as a boy, refused to leave Anfield. However, in

December 1969, the Golborne-born striker was persuaded to join Bolton in a £32,000 deal.

In an 11-season career at Anfield, he won two League Championship medals, a Second Division medal and an F.A. Cup Winners' medal.

He made his debut for Bolton in a Boxing Day win at Preston, but he could do little to revive the Wanderers' struggling fortunes. He did hit a hat-trick in a 3-0 win over Birmingham City, though Bolton were relegated to the Third Division for the first time in their history.

In April 1972, over 56,000 attended his testiomonial at Anfield to bid farewell to one of Liverpool's favourtie sons – one of the all-time great goalscorers.

MANCHESTER EVENING NEWS

LEIGHTON JAMES

Birthplace: Llwchwyr
Born: 16th February 1953
Position: Winger

Football League Career

	Appearances	Goals
Burnley	327 (1)	63
Derby County	67 (1)	15
Queen's Park Rangers	27 (1)	4
Swansea City	88 (10)	27
Sunderland	50 (2)	4
Bury	46	5
Newport County	21(7)	2
Total	626 (22)	120

Wales International Appearances	54
Goals	10

Arriving at Turf Moor from the Welsh town of Llwchwyr, Leighton James proved to be yet another outstanding product of the Burnley youth scheme.

He came into the Clarets' side during the 1970-71 season, when Burnley went down into the Second Division. Primarily a right-footed player, he played most of his games on the left wing. Like many wingers, he often felt that he didn't receive the protection he deserved and was occasionally seen complaining to the referee about the opposition!

At times, Leighton James was brilliant – a player of undeniable pace and skill. As well as setting up chances for others, he was quite capable of scoring goals and spectacular ones at that. He would cut in from the left flank and shoot with his favourite right foot – it was a great asset. James could drive the ball or curl it, the accuracy of his shooting also earning him a reputation as one of the game's best free-kick specialists. His best years were at Turf Moor, where he emerged alongside other Burnley youth team products like Ralph Coates, Martin Dobson and David Thomas. Unfortunately for Burnley and Lancashire football, James, like the other three, had to be sold to help balance the club's books. He had been at Turf Moor for five years and made 181 appearances before he signed for Derby County at a fee of £310,000 in 1975.

He spent two seasons at the Baseball Ground and one with Queen's Park Rangers before returning to Burnley in 1978.

He was by now an established Welsh international, having made his debut in the 1971-72 season, and he went on to play a total of 54 times for his country, scoring 10 goals.

A competent and shrewd player, you probably wouldn't have guessed that he was a professional footballer. For he wore glasses and had a very mild manner – yet on the field of play, he knew all the tricks!

In 1980, his Wales team-mate John Toshack signed him for Swansea City. Playing in his native country, James was a major influence in helping the Swans to reach the First Division for the first time in the club's history.
A crafty and temperamental player, he moved to the north-east, where he played in over 50 games for Sunderland, before spells with Bury and Newport County.
Known as 'Taffy' by the Burnley side, he returned to Turf Moor for a third time as player-coach in 1987. Nowadays, he can be heard as a TV commentator when the Welsh national side are playing.

LANCASHIRE EVENING TELEGRAPH

KEVIN KEEGAN

Birthplace:	Armthorpe, Nr Doncaster	
Born:	14th February 1951	
Position:	Forward	

Football League Career

	Appearances	Goals
Scunthorpe United	120 (4)	18
Liverpool	230	68
Southampton	68	37
Newcastle United	78	48
Total	496 (4)	171

England International Appearances	63
Goals	21

Kevin Keegan was born on St Valentine's Day in the small Yorkshire mining village of Armthorpe. He was turned down by Coventry City after a trial as a 15-year-old, for being too small. Determined to prove the doubters wrong, he returned home to play part-time football and was spotted by Scunthorpe United.

When Bill Shankly plucked him from the obscurity of the lower divisions in 1971, there were few who doubted the wisdom of the Liverpool manager's move. After three seasons playing with Scunthorpe United, Keegan was bought for £35,000 by Liverpool on 1st May 1971.

He hit Anfield like a tornado – converted from a deep-lying winger to striker, he made his debut against Notts Forest in the opening match of the 1971-72 season. He scored after seven minutes, serving notice that Shanks had found the missing link needed to inspire his rebuilt side. Normally, an unknown player like Keegan would have spent an apprenticeship in the reserves, but he had that rare kind of talent that was to turn him into a world-class star. His all-action approach won over the fans and he soon became the idol of the Kop. Bill Shankly called him "the player who ignited Liverpool" and he certainly was the star of many matches between 1971 and 1977.

Keegan was brave, quick and completely inexhaustible. His understanding up front with John Toshack appeared to border on telepathy.

His first three international appearances for England were all made against Wales; at Cardiff on 15th November 1972, at Wembley on 24th January 1973 and at Cardiff on 11th May 1974!

His performance in the 1974 F.A. Cup Final against Newcastle, when he scored two goals, was one of his best for the club. There were the odd turbulent times – sent off with Bremner at Wembley, and roughed up by the Belgrade police after walking out on England after being dropped by Don Revie.

The European Cup Final of 1977 against Borussia Moenchengladbach was Keegan's last game in the red of Liverpool. His duel with Bertie Vogts, captain of Borussia and West Germany, was a classic – Vogts was reckoned to

LIVERPOOL DAILY POST & ECHO

be the best at man-to-man marking, but Keegan ran him ragged. In 1977, he answered the call of continental football and joined S.V. Hamburg in Germany for £500,000. It made him England's most expensive and best-paid player.

During his six years at Anfield, he won three League Championship medals, two U.E.F.A. Cup winners' medals and European and F.A. Cup winners' medals.

His three years at Hamburg enhanced his game further, teaching him to overcome man-to-man marking. He had captained England and went on to twice become European Footballer of the Year. Keegan was an excellent finisher with good anticipation and acceleration, yet powerful in the air for someone of his height.

In February 1980, Southampton manager Lawrie McMenemy swooped to sign him, Keegan scoring 26 goals in the 1980-81 season. Those goals were sufficient to make Kevin the leading scorer in the First Division for which he was awarded the Shoot-Adidas Golden Boot.

Keegan made 63 appearances for his country, but didn't play for England after the 1982 World Cup, which was a shame, for he still had a lot of football in him as his two years with Newcastle United showed. He led them back into the First Division. Small he may have been, but in his day, Kevin Keegan was a footballing giant.

HOWARD KENDALL

Birthplace: Ryton-on-Tyne
Born: 22nd May 1946
Position: Midfield

Football League Career

	Appearances	Goals
Preston North End	104	13
Everton	231 (2)	21
Birmingham City	115	16
Stoke City	82	9
Blackburn Rovers	79	6
Total	611 (2)	65

Born at Ryton-on-Tyne on 22nd May 1946, Howard Kendall first played soccer at Unsworth Junior School, a school with a footballing tradition, for Jimmy Hagan, ex-Sheffield United and England, was an old boy.

After passing the 11-plus examination, he attended Washington Grammar School. As the seasons passed, he represented the Chester-le-Street district side, the Durham County team and then made a single appearance for England Schoolboys in a 7-3 win over Wales at Swansea.

In August 1961, he went south to become a Preston apprentice. He made his League debut in his native north-east, 11 days before his 17th birthday as North End drew 2-2 with Newcastle. His first League goal came later that season at the Dell as Preston beat Southampton 5-4 in a nine goal thriller.

At the age of 17 years 345 days, he became the youngest player ever to appear in a Cup Final (a record since surpassed by Paul Allen, then of West Ham and now of Spurs), but First Division West Ham ran out winners 3-2.

During 1964-65, Kendall was chosen for an F.A. team under Alf Ramsey that made a two-match tour of Gibraltar; the side won both games, Kendall scoring in each of them.

In March 1967, Harry Catterick paid Preston £80,000 for the 21-year-old. At Goodison, he became a member of the legendary midfield trio of Kendall, Ball and Harvey. He picked up another loser's medal in the 1968 Cup Final, but in 1969-70 won a League Championship medal.

A wing-half from the old school, he was a steady passer, defended well and made good forward runs, but didn't score many goals. He collected Football League representative honours and Under-23 caps and was unlucky not to have got into the senior side. He was good enough to have played for England, for at times when he was with Everton, his influence in midfield was quite awesome.

In February 1974 he was part of a complex transfer package which took Bob Latchford from Birmingham City to Everton while Kendall made the opposite journey. He proved a reliable buy for the St Andrews outfit, helping to stabilize them in the First Division and also taking them to the 1975 F.A. Cup semi-final.

In August 1977, he joined Stoke City for £40,000 and became club coach under Alan Durban as Stoke won promotion to Division One in 1978-79. During the 1979 close season, he arrived at Blackburn as player-manager. During his time at Ewood it was his performances on the field as much as anything else which helped take the club from the Third Division to the brink of the First within two seasons. Despite entering the veteran stage of his career, he showed all the determination and drive of his earlier days, dictating play and inspiring those around him. It was perhaps the least surprising event in his career, when in the summer of 1981 he returned to Goodison as player-manager. He had his problems in those early days, but eventually got it right, steering the Toffees to Championship wins in 1985 and 1987.

LIVERPOOL DAILY POST & ECHO

Significantly this upsurge in the form of Everton conincided with the appointment of Colin Harvey as first-team coach. They now enjoyed a new lease of life in management. However, after the League Championship win of 1987, Howard felt he could do no more and was enticed to Athletico Bilbao in Spain. He eventually returned to manage the troubled Manchester City and kept them in the First Division. When Colin Harvey (who'd replaced Kendall at Everton in 1987) was dismissed, it left the door open for Kendall to return to his beloved Goodison for a third time.

BRIAN LABONE

Birthplace:	Liverpool
Born:	23rd January 1940
Position:	Centre-Half

Football League Career

	Appearances	Goals
Everton	451	2
Total	451	2

England International Appearances	26
Goals	0

Brian Labone came to prominence in April 1957, a month after leaving the Liverpool Collegiate. He had been pondering over whether to go on to University or to become a professional footballer – football won. Signing for Everton, he gained an immediate place in the Central League side, avoiding the junior teams – it was a tremendous step from the Merseyside Grammar Schools side.

Everton's regular centre-half, Tommy T E Jones, was injured and Labone came in for his first-team debut at St Andrews against Birmingham City on March 25th 1958 at the age of 18.

One of the game's great competitors, he was only booked twice in 530 first-team appearances, playing against some of the game's roughest and toughest strikers in the country. After opposing some of the game's toughest centre-forwards, men like Andy Lochhead (Burnley) and Bobby Smith (Tottenham Hotspur), he found that strikers became much more subtle as the old formation was replaced by 4 – 2 – 4. Everton now operated with twin centre-backs and that was the time that John Hurst joined him in the heart of the Everton defence.

Labone won the first of his 26 England caps in October 1962, playing against Northern Ireland in Belfast. He was only 22 years old and was the first Everton player since the war to be capped – a great achievement.

In 1966, he had a great chance of being England's World Cup centre-half, but he made a shock request to be overlooked in order that he could go ahead with his planned summer marriage to a former Miss Liverpool! That news soon took a back seat as Labone fulfilled his boyhood dream and led the Blues to victory in the F.A. Cup Final against Sheffield Wednesday.

Just sixteen months after that Wembley success, he dropped a bombshell by announcing his retirement. He revealed that he wasn't enjoying his football and would be quitting at the end of his contract or earlier, if Everton could find a suitable replacement.

Having made the announcement, he then began to produce some of his best ever football and was recalled into the England squad. Some sixteen months later, he announced he would be staying on to allow Everton to use his ability and experience to the full in a team of very promising youngsters. He was a key figure when the Championship title returned to Goodison in 1970, a season in which he played for the 500th time, in the match against Southampton on January 17th.

One of the greatest of club men, he was a pillar in the Everton defence for fifteen seasons. It was reckoned that there was no safer sight in football than to see Brian Labone marshalling his defenders. A great leader, he captained a Football League XI against the Irish and led an F.A. Select side in Canada.

Brian Labone was one of the old school of footballers, surviving the football revolution to remain the model professional. He finished his career on 24th August 1971, finishing just 12 games short of Ted Sagar's, Everton's immortal 'keeper's, all-time record.

He was forced to quit the game after an Achilles tendon injury. A fine example of a man dedicated to his sport – his loss was a shattering blow for Everton and one that they felt for the next decade.

LIVERPOOL DAILY POST & ECHO

BOBBY LANGTON

Birthplace:	Burscough
Born:	8th September 1918
Position:	Outside-Left

Football League Career

	Appearances	Goals
Blackburn Rovers	212	57
Preston North End	55	14
Bolton Wanderers	118	16
Total	385	87

England International Appearances	11
Goals	1

Bobby Langton was a promising teenager, who signed for Blackburn Rovers for just £50 from Southport League side, Burscough Victoria, in 1937. At the time, he was only 18 years old, but was quickly installed into the outside-left position, from where he scored 14 goals in 37 appearances during Rovers' promotion campaign of 1938-39. His First Division appearances were restricted to three, scoring the second equaliser in the 2-2 draw with Everton in the last game before the outbreak of war interrupted his career.

During the war, he was an infantryman in India and represented the Army in practically every game they played during his service. He appeared in the 1940 War Cup Final when Rovers lost 0-1 to West Ham. In 1945, he was a member of the Glentoran team that reached the Irish Cup Final and also represented the Irish League against the Combined Services in Belfast.

The end of the war saw him restored to the Blackburn side and in September 1946, he won his first cap for England against Northern Ireland.

Blackburn's fortunes waned and in August 1949, he was transferred to Preston North End for £16,000. In the same month, he netted a goal after only seven seconds from the kick-off against Manchester City. In November 1949, Bobby Langton was on his way to Bolton Wanderers, for what was then a club record fee of £20,000.

Langton was in his prime – possessing a very powerful shot, he liked to cut inside from the left and have a crack at goal. He was a speedy winger who could put in crosses from all angles.

At Bolton, he became a regular in the number 11 shirt until 1953, when he was placed on the transfer list at his own request. He remained long enough to play in the 1953 F.A. Cup Final against Blackpool. In September of that year, he returned to Ewood Park.

Although his speed had diminished somewhat in his second spell at Blackburn, he added a great deal of guile and cunning to his play. In fact, in his second spell with the Rovers, he scored 33 goals from his 105 appearances.

After leaving League football, he had a spell in Ireland with Ards, before entering non-League football with Kidderminster Harriers. His non-League career took him to Wisbech Town, twice (where he became a publican) and Colwyn Bay. In 1962, he became trainer-coach at King's Lynn and a year later took over a similar position at Wisbech. Five years later, he returned to his roots, becoming manager of Burscough Rangers.

WALLY & HOWARD TALBOT PHOTOGRAPHY

BOB LATCHFORD

Birthplace:	Birmingham
Born:	18th January 1951
Position:	Centre-Forward

Football League Career

	Appearances	Goals
Birmingham City	158 (2)	68
Everton	235 (1)	106
Swansea City	87	35
Coventry City	11 (1)	2
Lincoln City	14 (1)	2
Newport County	20	5
Total	525 (5)	218

England International Appearances	12
Goals	5

Brought up in Birmingham, Bob Latchford atended Brandwood School in King's Heath, signing for Birmingham City as an outside-left in 1966. He was soon moved to the middle of the attack and given his League debut on March 21st 1969 against Preston North End. He made a very encouraging start to his League career, Birmingham winning 3-2, Latchford scoring with two headers, one in each half.

He had scored 68 goals in 158 appearances for the Midlands side when in February 1974, Everton manager Billy Bingham paid a record fee of £350,000 for their centre-forward. In return, Howard Kendall and Archie Styles went in the opposite direction.

He took a little time to feel at home at Goodison, but once he did, the goals started to flow.

A strong, burly centre-forward, he was a difficult man to shake off the ball and was a fine header. He had the special knack of turning half chances into goals. He was Everton's leading goalscorer for four consecutive seasons from 1975.

I was at Burnden Park on February 15th 1977, when Bob Latchford scored the only goal of the Football League Cup semi-final Second Leg to send the Blues to Wembley after Bolton had battled hard for a 1-1 draw at Goodison.

At the outset of the 1977-78 campaign, the Daily Express announced that they were awarding £10,000 for the first player in the top two divisions of the Football League to reach 30 goals. In October of that season, Latchford scored four goals when Everton beat Q.P.R. 5-1 at Loftus Road. He also hit a hat-trick in a 6-0 home victory over Coventry City, with ex-Burnley winger Dave Thomas providing the crosses.

On April 29th 1978, Latchford scored the two goals he needed to become the first top-flight player for six years to score 30 goals, in a 6-0 thrashing of Chelsea. It was a close call, for there were only eight minutes of the season left!

Latchford didn't receive anywhere near £10,000 – just

£192 to be exact! It was part of the deal that £5,000 went to the Football League and Professional Footballers' Association Benevolent Fund; Bob shared the rest between all the players who had helped him to achieve his 30-goal haul.

Also that season, he made his full England debut in the World Cup qualifying match against Italy at Wembley. He appeared 12 times for his country, only appearing on the losing side in his last match against Austria.

In the 1978-79 season, he scored a stunning five goals as Everton trounced Wimbledon in a League Cup match. He remained at Goodison for a further three seasons after that memorable 30-goal season.

When Howard Kendall returned to Everton as player-manager, Latchford was the first to depart, joining Swansea City for a fee of £125,000. In 286 games for the Blues, he had scored 138 goals to make him the club's leading goalscorer since the war. His goals had given Everton supporters a great deal of pleasure.

LIVERPOOL DAILY POST & ECHO

DENIS LAW

Birthplace:	Aberdeen
Born:	24th February 1940
Position:	Forward

Football League Career

	Appearances	Goals
Huddersfield Town	81	16
Manchester City	66 (2)	30
Manchester United	305 (4)	171
Total	452 (6)	217

Scotland International Appearances	55
Goals	30

Denis Law was one of the great strikers and characters in the modern game, yet when he arrived at Huddersfield Town from Aberdeen in 1956, he was a thin bespectacled 16-year-old who looked nothing like a footballer.

Educated at Hilton Primary, Kittybrewster Junior and Powis Secondary Modern Schools in Aberdeen, Law signed professional forms for Huddersfield on 25th February 1957. The following year, he became Scotland's youngest player in modern times at 18 years 236 days when he made his debut against Wales.

He stayed with the Yorkshire club until March 1960, when Manchester City paid Huddersfield £55,000 for his services. It was a League record fee, surpassing the previous British transfer record by £10,000. On 28th January 1961, Denis Law produced a display of a lifetime to score six goals in a fourth-round F.A. Cup tie, only for the referee to abandon the game with 21 minutes to play. Luton Town were the opponents at Kenilworth Road, racing into a two-goal lead within the first eighteen minutes. However, before half-time, Law had completed his hat-trick and within 25 minutes of the second-half, he had collected a second hat-trick! His six goals had come in 48 minutes but the conditions were worsening and the referee ended the game. A few days later, when it was replayed, City lost 3-1, with that man Law scoring again.

On 13th July 1961, Italian giants Torino paid £100,000 for Law's skills. It was the first time that a British club had been involved in a six-figure transfer. Twelve months later, he joined Manchester United, when they became the first British club to pay over £100,000 for a player.

Denis Law was unselfish in setting up goals for team-mates, yet he had a killer instinct himself and in the six-yard box, he was electric. He could score goals from impossible situations. His blond hair and one arm raised to salute a goal helped establish the Law legend.

He scored on his United debut in August 1962 as the Reds drew 2-2 at West Brom. On 3rd November 1962, he scored 4 goals for Manchester United against Ipswich and then four days later, scored a further 4 goals for Scotland against Norway. A year earlier, he had scored 4 goals for Scotland against Northern Ireland. Law rounded off a superb first season by scoring at Wembley as United beat Leicester City 3-1.

Denis Law claims the existing record for the most hat-tricks to have been scored in European Cup competitions by anyone for a Football League Cup. With Manchester United, he recorded five: two each in the European Cup and Cup-Winners Cup and one in the Fairs Cup. Soon his goals, in between lengthy bouts of suspension as he rebelled against the increasingly harsh treatment he was receiving, were inspiring United to two League Championships, but unfortunately, he had to watch United's 4-1 win over Benfica in the 1968 European Cup Final from his hospital bed after a knee operation.

Though his disciplinary record stopped him from being voted Footballer of the Year, the English soccer writers' counterparts on the continent voted him European Footballer of the Year in 1964, a well deserved award.

He never reached the same heights again, but did enjoy an Indian summer with Manchester City as he returned to Maine Road in July 1973. He made another Wembley appearance with City and at the close of his international career, at last enjoyed a trip to the World Cup in Germany in 1974, by which time he was 34. Ironically, his last League goal was a cheeky back-heel, consigning United to the Second Division – never had he taken less pleasure with a goal.

Now a commentator for BBC Radio, at Old Trafford he found his natural, spiritual home and his goals lit up a decade for United and Scotland.

MANCHESTER EVENING NEWS

FRANCIS LEE

Birthplace:	Westhoughton
Born:	29th April 1944
Position:	Forward

Football League Career

	Appearances	Goals
Bolton Wanderers	189	92
Manchester City	248 (1)	112
Derby County	62	24
Total	499 (1)	228

England International Appearances	27
Goals	10

Francis Lee made his League debut for Bolton Wanderers as a 16-year-old amateur in November 1960, after playing in only eight Central League games. He partnered 35-year-old Nat Lofthouse on the right-wing in a 3-1 victory over Manchester City at Burnden Park. It was an eventful debut for the young star, Lee scoring a goal and getting booked.

He signed professional forms for the Wanderers in May 1961, but his volatile nature caused problems off the field when he refused to play after being dropped to the Bolton 'A' team.

Things were patched up and though clubs were keen to sign him, following a string of transfer requests, Lee stayed with Bolton until the beginning of the 1967-68 season.

In October 1967 at the age of 23, he signed for Manchester City and made his League debut against Wolverhampton Wanderers. During his eight years with Bolton, he had scored over 100 goals and was rarely out of the headlines. He soon became a firm favourite with the Maine Road fans and was one of the successes in a City team that enjoyed one of the greatest eras in the club's history.

By the time he went to City, he was playing a more orthodox striking role. 'Franny' Lee was a bustling, sturdy little striker. He had a barrel chest and though slightly portly, he was one of the most tenacious and effective of strikers, scoring many goals. He hit three hat-tricks in his years at Maine Road, including a spectacular threesome in the Manchester derby of 1970-71. His others came in the 5-2 thrashing of Wolverhampton Wanderers in January 1972 and in a 4-0 win over Walsall, a League Cup Second Round replay played at Old Trafford, after the first two matches hadn't produced a goal. Francis Lee won a lot of penalties for City and wasn't really too fussy about how he won them. City won so many penalties during the early 1970s it became a topical talking point. In fact, many of them were awarded for fouls against Franny.

In the European Cup-Winners Final of 1970 against Gornik Zabrze of Poland, he hit the ball so hard and straight into the net, that it needed a close study of an

MANCHESTER EVENING NEWS

action-replay to check the ball had not gone through Kostka the goal-keeper's body!

In 1971-72, Lee topped the Division One goalscorers for City with 33 goals, including 15 from the penalty spot – a record! For this achievement he was awarded the bronze boot in the Golden Boot Competition.

Lee was also a vital part of Sir Alf Ramsey's England squad and had gone to Mexico to defend the World Cup in 1970. He scored 10 goals in 27 appearances for England.

After scoring 112 goals for Manchester City in his 248 League appearances, he joined Derby County in August 1974 for £110,000 -without doubt, one of Dave Mackay's best ever signings. He won a second Championship medal at the Baseball Ground and added 24 League goals to his tally before retiring in 1976.

By then, his paper business which he started whilst a player with Bolton Wanderers was a great success and eventually secured him millionaire status. Also, having obtained a licence in 1986, he became a breeder and trainer of racehorses near his Cheshire home.

BILLY LIDDELL

Birthplace:	Dunfermline
Born:	10th January 1922
Position:	Forward

Football League Career

	Appearances	Goals
Liverpool	495	216
Total	495	216

Scotland International Appearances	28
Goals	6

Billy Liddell joined Liverpool as an 18-year-old from the Fifeshire junior club, Lochgelly Violet. He started learning his trade in the English game in the Lancashire Mid-Week League, only to see the first six years of his career lost to the war. Though he served as an R.A.F. navigator, he played almost 150 times for his club, as football continued on a regional basis. He hit a powerful hat-trick against another Lancashire 'Great' Frank Swift in a 7-3 win over Manchester City.

His reputation as a flying winger with a powerful shot in either foot was growing and Liddell made eight appearances for his country in wartime internationals.

He didn't make his official Liverpool debut until 5th January 1946. He was just five days short of his 24th birthday as he scored in an F.A. Cup Third Round tie against Chester.

However, it was on the restart of League Football that Billy Liddell's career began to take off. In 1946-47, he played in 35 games as Liverpool won the first post-war Championship. He revealed the pace and power that were to be his hallmark for almost 15 years. He only scored 7 goals, but showed the dashing style that was to make him one of Liverpool's most prolific goalscorers. In 1949-50, Liverpool were unbeaten in their opening 19 matches, setting a record in a 42-match season. During that run, Liddell was at his best, creating havoc amongst opposition defences and scoring goals. In one five-match spell, he scored in every game.

Unfortunately, he didn't add an F.A. Cup winners' medal to it, for Arsenal beat the Reds 2-0 in the 1950 Final. He was, along with Stanley Matthews, one of two players to play in both the Great Britain v Rest of World and Rest of Europe matches.

When Liverpool were relegated to the Second Division at the end of the 1953-54 season, his reaction was typical of the man. He showed great determination and in his first four seasons out of the top flight, he scored 101 goals in 156 League matches.

He could torture defences – take your eyes off him for a moment and the chances were that you would pay with a goal. He was a prolific scorer for a winger, averaging a dozen goals a season. He was so popular and had such an immense influence on the side, that the fans re-christened

WALLY & HOWARD TALBOT PHOTOGRAPHY

the club 'Liddellpool' and made Billy Liddell their 'King'!

A vital member of the Scottish national side, he made 28 appearances between 1946 and 1955.

During Billy Liddell's last season, the attendances at Anfield started to slump. Almost 44,000 had watched the opening match, but only 13,000 watched the final home gate. The loyalty of the fans towards Billy Liddell remained unchanged, as over 38,000 paid tribute to him in a benefit match between Liverpool and an all-star team.

Billy Liddell set a wonderful example to any young player aspiring to greatness and on his retirement, he became a bursar at Liverpool University, after studying accountancy throughout his playing career. He was also appointed a Justice of the Peace and undertook a great amount of work for boys' clubs.

In 16 seasons, he made a grand total of 537 first-team appearances and scored 299 goals. In the course of building up these statistics, Billy Liddell became one of the greatest Anfield heroes of all time.

NAT LOFTHOUSE

Birthplace:	Bolton
Born:	27th August 1925
Position:	Centre-Forward

Football League Career

	Appearances	Goals
Bolton Wanderers	452	255
Total	452	255

England International Appearances	33
Goals	30

Nat Lofthouse recalled that his first game of football was as an emergency goalkeeper and when he returned home, it was to be given a severe lecture from his parents for kicking out a brand-new pair of shoes!

Attending the same school as the legendary Tommy Lawton, he signed for Bolton Wanderers in 1939, after having played for Bolton Schools XI and Lomax's, a team in the Lancashire combination.

His first game for the Wanderers was in March 1941, when at the age of 15 years 207 days, he scored twice as Bolton beat Bury 5-1 at Burnden Park in a Football League North game. The son of a Bolton coalman, he worked on the coalface during the war years, often going straight from the pit to assist the Wanderers in wartime games. He was on the field in March 1946, when 33 people lost their lives in the Burnden disaster. Nat was recognised at international level in November 1950 when he was chosen to lead England's forward line at Highbury in the match against Yugoslavia. He fulfilled his promise by scoring both England's goals in a 2-2 draw in a game that was to be the first of a glittering career for England.

In May 1952, he earned the tag of 'Lion of Vienna' after his heroic performances against Austria, when he scored twice in England's 3-2 win. The winning goal came nine minutes from time, as he collected a pass from Tom Finney and began a surging run that took him from the halfway line to the Austrian penalty area. As the Austrian goalkeeper charged out at him, Nat didn't falter and hit the ball cleanly into the corner of the net – the impact was such that when he and the goalkeeper collided, Nat had to leave the field for treatment. In September 1952, he scored six goals for the Football League against the Irish League at Molineux.

He scored in every round of the 1952-53 F.A. Cup competition, but injury-hit Bolton lost 4-3 to Blackpool in the final. He was voted Footballer of the Year at the end of that season by the Football Writers' Association. In 1955-56, he was the leading goalscorer in the First Division with 33 goals.

In 1958, he captained Bolton to their F.A. Cup victory over Manchester United, scoring both goals in Wanderers' 2-0 win. His second became a major talking point, when he charged both the ball and United's Irish 'keeper Harry

Gregg over the goal-line.

On October 22nd 1958, Nat played his last game for England. He was recalled for the first time since 1956, his powerful running causing some anxious moments in the Russian defence. England were coasting at 4-0, when in the last minute, Bobby Charlton found the big man with a good pass. The Bolton centre-forward fired in a splendid shot for the fifth goal, much to the delight of the crowd – it brought the loudest cheer of the afternoon.

He won 33 caps and scored what was then a record 30 goals for his country. After an injury in the club's South African tour, he missed the entire 1959-60 season, but in typical fashion he fought back to regain his place. On December 17th 1960, he received a leg injury in Bolton's 2-2 draw at Birmingham that finally ended his illustrious playing career. One of his last goals for the club came the previous month in a 3-1 home win over Manchester City.

He was then appointed assistant trainer and in 1967 became chief coach. He succeeded Bill Ridding as manager, but left the club in 1971. He returned to become executive club manager and later president to continue his devotion to Lancashire's oldest club.

MANCHESTER EVENING NEWS

Nat Lofthouse is undoubtedly Bolton Wanderers' most illustrious personality – he was the Trotters' post-war hero.

TERRY McDERMOTT

Birthplace:	Kirkby
Born:	8th December 1951
Position:	Midfield

Football League Career

	Appearances	Goals
Bury	83 (7)	8
Newcastle United	129 (1)	18
Liverpool	221 (11)	54
Total	433 (19)	80

England International Appearances	25
Goals	3

Though Liverpool-born, Terry McDermott began his footballing career with homely Bury, for whom he made 90 League appearances before his transfer to Newcastle United.

Although on the losing side in the 1974 F.A. Cup Final against Liverpool, Terry McDermott had been particularly impressive for the Magpies. Within a matter of months, he had been transferred to Anfield for a fee of £170,000. He went straight into the Liverpool side, but failed to settle as the Reds' new manager Bob Paisley experimented in an attempt to continue where Bill Shankly had left off. Liverpool won the League Championship and the U.E.F.A. Cup in 1975-76 without McDermott's assistance and it seemed only a matter of time before his arrival would be written off as an expensive mistake and he was transferred. However, Bob Paisley kept faith with him and the following season saw him firmly established by the spring, playing a memorable role in the run-in, which saw the League title and European Cup come to Anfield, but the F.A. Cup go to Old Trafford. He was superb and dangerous when running from deep positions and arriving late in the penalty area, where his finishing could be deadly. That campaign saw him score two really outstanding goals. The first came at Maine Road in the F.A. Cup semi-final against Everton, as he spotted goalkeeper David Lawson off his line and chipped in a beautiful goal. The second was probably the most important goal of his career. It broke the deadlock in the 1977 European Cup Final against Borussia Moenchengladbach in Rome. He ghosted down the inside-right channel to receive Steve Heighway's pass and curl the ball in superb fashion round the German 'keeper.

It was the following year, when Graeme Souness arrived at Anfield that McDermott reached his peak. The Scot's style of play allowed the wiry McDermott the freedom he needed to express his talents fully. He covered every inch of grass on the pitch, often acting as a decoy and creating space for his colleagues to exploit. When in possession, his control and instinctive passing ability allowed him to get the best out of the situation.

In September 1978, he started and finished one of Anfield's

best ever goals in the televised 7-0 hammering of Spurs. In 1979-80, he was the club's top scorer with 13 goals, hitting a hat-trick against Oulu Palloseura, the Finnish champions, in a 10-1 victory.

In 1980, he became the first man to win awards from the Football Writers and his fellow players in the same season.

He made another valuable contribution in 1981-82, getting 14 goals in 28 games as Liverpool won the League title and Milk Cup.

He seemed to lose a little impetus and returned to the north-east to team up with Kevin Keegan at Newcastle, as the Magpies staged a revival. A happy-go-lucky midfield player, he ended his playing days with Cork City and Apoel, Cyprus.

LIVERPOOL DAILY POST & ECHO

JIMMY McILROY

Birthplace: Lambeg
Born: 25th October 1931
Position: Inside-Forward

Football League Career

	Appearances	Goals
Burnley	439	116
Stoke City	96 (2)	16
Oldham Athletic	35 (1)	1
Total	570 (3)	133

Northern Ireland International Appearances	55
Goals	10

Burnley have always been noted for their ability to find stars without breaking the bank, but they can not have made a better investment than the £7,000 they paid Glentoran for Jimmy McIlroy.

Born at Lambeg near Belfast, he made his senior debut with Glentoran in the last game of the 1948-49 season as well as winning Irish Youth international honours.

At Burnley he became recognised as one of the most accomplished inside-forwards of the post-war era. Northern Ireland capped him for the first time in October 1951 and he subsequently enjoyed one run of 34 consecutive appearances.

McIlroy was a natural player, rarely caught in possession – a cool performer with plenty of time on the ball. His great strength was the consistency of service to the centre-forward and largely because of that, he became the architect of the great Burnley side of the late 1950s and early 1960s. In August 1955, he was inside-left in Great Britain's team that played against the Rest of Europe.

McIlroy was an intelligent playmaker, a classical scheming inside-forward. He enjoyed splendid partnerships with Jimmy Adamson for Burnley and Danny Blanchflower for Northern Ireland. With Docherty as manager, McIlroy and Blanchflower masterminded Northern Ireland to their greatest heights in the 1958 World Cup. They reached the quarter-finals with McIlroy forming a devastating partnership with Peter McParland, the Aston Villa winger. McIlroy's influence played a major role in Burnley's Championship triumph of 1960. After winning a League Championship medal and an F.A. Cup Finalists' medal with Burnley and appearing in over 400 Division One games for the Clarets, most people thought he was going to end his playing career with the Turf Moor outfit, but there was a shock when he signed for Stoke City for £25,000 in March 1963 after being placed on the transfer list.

When he left Burnley, they were one of the top clubs in the country and his reputation must have helped them to attract many of the good young players who were later to become the life-blood of the club and give them one of the most productive youth schemes in the country.

He made an immediate impression on his arrival at the Victoria Ground, helping the Potters to clinch the Second Division title in 1962-63. He played 100 games for Stoke before moving to Oldham Athletic for a brief spell before retiring. This new found form with Stoke, led to him being recalled into the Northern Ireland team in 1966 after a three year gap. He represented his country on 55 occasions, scoring 10 goals, including one in Northern Ireland's historic victory at Wembley in 1957.

After finishing his career back in Lancashire with Oldham, he moved to Stoke City as chief coach. He resigned his position there in 1969 and was out of the game until 4th November 1970 when he was appointed team manager at Bolton. Incredibly, after only 18 days in charge, McIlroy parted company with the club. He returned to Burnley, where he still fills the post of sports journalist.

WALLY & HOWARD TALBOT PHOTOGRAPHY

SAMMY McILROY

Birthplace:	Belfast
Born:	2nd August 1954
Position:	Midfield

Footbal League Career

	Appearances	Goals
Manchester United	320 (22)	57
Stoke City	132 (1)	14
Manchester City	13	1
Bury	50 (5)	6
Preston North End	20	0
Total	535 (28)	78

Northern Ireland International Appearances	88
Goals	5

Matt Busby signed the Belfast-born Sammy McIlroy as an apprentice professional on his 15th birthday and he became a full-timer exactly two years later. Despite the managerial upheavals and boardroom in-fighting, McIlroy stayed true to the Reds – no tantrums, transfer requests or walkouts.

He made his debut for United in November 1971 just three months after his 17th birthday, in front of 63,000 fans at Maine Road in the Manchester derby. He had been called in to deputise for the injured Denis Law. No place for the inexperienced youngster, you might think. Far from it – United and City split the points in a 3-3 thriller and young McIlroy hit the Reds' first goal with all the confidence of a seasoned professional.

Even though Denis returned, he kept his place for the following game against Tottenham Hotspur and socred in a 3-1 win which kept United on top of the First Division.

Most united fans would agree that Sammy McIlroy didn't quite rank alongside Best, Charlton and Law, but he developed different and equally important qualities – loyalty and consistency. Year in, year out, whether in attack or midfield, the gifted Northern Irishman turned in consistently excellent performances.

In February 1972, he lined up with George Best for his international debut against Spain – a 1-1 draw played in the unusual setting of Hull City's Boothferry Park ground because of the 'troubles' in Ulster. McIlroy was also badly hurt in a car crash in 1973, which kept him out of action for six months.

At United, McIlroy showed his ability to take on defenders, his bursts down the flanks leading to United's attacks and his happy knack of scoring important goals.

United stormed to the Second Division title at the first attempt – McIlroy was an ever-present. In their first season back in the top flight, they finished third and reached the F.A. Cup Final, helped by 10 McIlroy goals.

He often made a habit of scoring stunning goals, like the one against Liverpool in 1977-78 – a thundering volley, or the superb jinking run and shot from the edge of the box which rocked Albion at Old Trafford in December of the same season. His most memorable goal must be the one he scored in the 1979 F.A. Cup Final against Arsenal – a jinking run through a packed Gunners' penalty area and a curling shot past his international team-mate Pat Jennings, brought United back into a game which seemed lost beyond recall.

He won 88 international caps, playing an important role in Billy Bingham's team, which was to become one of the most successful in the country's history. He was virtually an ever-present as Northern Ireland twice won the Home International Championships and went to successive World Cup finals in 1982 and 1986, captaining the side in the latter tournament.

He had left United by then, moving to the Victoria Ground in February 1982 for a fee of £350,000. In 1984-85, he played some of his best football in a struggling Stoke side, but at the end of that season, he was given a free transfer by the relegated Potters. He returned to Manchester to play for City, but it was a grave mistake, as he was still regarded a Red.

A forceful, hard-working midfield player, he ended his first-class playing days with Bury and Preston North End.

MANCHESTER EVENING NEWS

SIR STANLEY MATTHEWS

Birthplace:	Hanley
Born:	1st February 1915
Position:	Winger

Football League Career

	Appearances	Goals
Stoke City	82	7
Blackpool	379	17
Total	461	24

England International Appearances	54
Goals	11

Known as the 'Wizard of Dribble' because of his close ball control, Stanley Matthews was the biggest crowd-puller in the 1950s. Born in Hanley, the son of a boxing barber, he started off as an outstanding schoolboy footballer, beginning as a centre-half, but switching to the right-wing and becoming an apprentice at Stoke City.

He made his League debut for Stoke on 19th March 1932 against Bury at Gigg Lane, and helped the Potters win promotion to the First Division in his second season. The following year, he made his international debut for England against Wales. He won a total of 54 caps, not including war-time and victory appearances for England. His fame grew quickly, fans trooping to matches in their thousands just to watch the 'Wizard of Dribble'.

Matthews liked the ball played to his feet. Stopping it dead and with perfect control, he shuffled towards the full-back, teasing him with the ball. The full-back very rarely committed himself, fearing Matthews' reputation. Stan would approach slowly, swaying his body from side to side. The defender would retreat until he thought he knew the direction in which Matthews was going and then lunge for the ball. But Matthews had gone, switching the ball to the opposite side and sprinting down the wing. However, he was more than just a master of dribble – with just one glance, he could deliver an inch-perfect pass.

When Matthews first asked Stoke for a transfer in 1938, there was a public outcry. Over 3,000 fans attended a protest meeting and another 1,000 paraded outside the ground with placards – he stayed. However, when he did move on to Blackpool in 1947, it was for the bargain price of £11,500.

There is also a little known fact, that among Stan's trophies there is a Cup medal that he won with Glasgow Rangers in a war-time game against Partick Thistle, Rangers winning 3-0.

He played for Blackpool in the 1948 F.A. Cup Final and was on the losing side, though there was consolation for him in being elected Britain's first Footballer of the Year. It was the same story against Newcastle in 1951 and in 1953 – it looked like being a third losers' medal with 20 minutes to go, when Blackpool trailed Bolton 3-1. But Matthews turned on a brilliant display and tore apart the

Bolton defence. Blackpool won 4-3 and the match, one of the greatest seen at Wembley, is hailed as the 'Matthews Cup Final'.

When England entered their first World Cup tournament in 1950, Stanley Matthews was already 35 years old. He had been a League footballer for 18 years and an international for 16, yet he went to Rio and played against Spain. Perhaps even more remarkable, he played in the 1954 finals as well. When England beat Scotland 7-2 at Wembley in 1955, the 40-year-old Matthews made five of the goals. It was Duncan Edwards' international debut – when Matthews first played for England, Edwards had not been born!

In 1956, he was voted European Footballer of the Year and awarded the O.B.E. the following year.

WALLY & HOWARD TALBOT PHOTOGRAPHY

Matthews returned to Stoke in 1961 and the fans flooded back through the gates of the Victoria Ground. He helped Stoke into the First Division and when he played his 701st and last game against Fulham on 6th February 1965, he was 50 years and 5 days. He was also knighted this year, the first footballer to be so honoured.

After he retired, he went to live in Malta, where he coached Hibernian (he also played for them until he was 55 years old). He also played for local sides and was still sprinting down the wing in his 60s. Stan Matthews was a difficult man to incorporate in a team pattern and there have been doubts about how he would have coped in the modern game, when he would rarely have been left one-to-one with a full-back and when he would have been expected to tackle back.

There will of course never be unanimous agreement on the name of the best player who ever lived or even the name of the best British player, but one thing is certain, that the name of Sir Stanley Matthews would figure largely in those discussions.

WILLIE MORGAN

Birthplace:	Sauchie, Near Alloa
Born:	2nd October 1944
Position:	Winger; Midfield

Football League Career

	Appearances	Goals
Burnley	195 (1)	19
Manchester United	236 (2)	24
Bolton Wanderers	154 (1)	10
Blackpool	41 (1)	4
Total	626 (5)	57

Scotland International Appearances	21
Goals	1

A Scottish Schoolboy trialist when playing for Fishcross Boys' Club at Sauchie, near Alloa in 1959, he signed as an amateur for Burnley in May 1960. He turned professional the following year, but had to wait until 1963 before he made his first-team debut against Sheffield Wednesday. He won the first of his 21 caps for Scotland in October 1967 against Northern Ireland.

By now, his wing play was attracting the attention of a number of clubs and he decided that he needed to leave Burnley to benefit his career. The club refused his transfer request and so his own game began to deteriorate. His lowest ebb must have been when the Burnley club refused to let him play in any of the sides and banned him from the training ground.

However, in August 1968, Manchester United paid £117,000 to take him to Old Trafford, where he won the remainder of his international caps.

Although not renowned for his goalscoring ability, Morgan nevertheless created many for Best, Charlton, Law, Macari and Pearson. He did a hat-trick in his first season, as United beat Queen's Park Rangers 8-1 at Old Trafford. It was United boss Frank O'Farrell who converted Morgan into a midfield role, from where he helped the Reds to take the Second Division title in 1974-75.

He returned to Burnley in the 1975 close season, but only managed a further 12 appearances before joining Bolton in March 1976 at the age of 31. He had returned to Turf Moor along with Mike Summerbee because manager Jimmy Adamson believed in playing attacking football, but within six months, Adamson was on his way to Sunderland.

The Bolton fans had already seen another 'old-winger' in Peter Thompson turn on the style and they certainly expected nothing less from Willie Morgan. He didn't disappoint them and missed only three games in between his debut against Plymouth Argyle and May 1979. During his time at Bolton, they became one of the classiest sides in the Second Division and won the title in 1977-78, when Morgan missed only one game.

In November 1978, Morgan was at the centre of a court

sensation, when Tommy Docherty, his former manager at United, brought a libel action against him and Granada TV. The action collapsed when Docherty admitted that he had lied in court.

Whilst at Bolton, he twice played in the N.A.S.L. for Minnesota Kicks and Vancouver Whitecaps. His last game in Bolton's colours came at Old Trafford in February 1980, the Reds winning 2-0. In September 1980 he moved to Bloomfield Road, where he played in 41 League games for the Seasiders.

He then had a further spell with Minnesota Kicks, retiring in May 1982 at the age of 37, with well over 725 senior games to his credit.

MANCHESTER EVENING NEWS

STAN MORTENSEN

Birthplace:	South Shields
Born:	26th May 1921
Position:	Forward

Football League Career

	Appearances	Goals
Blackpool	317	197
Hull City	42	18
Southport	36	10
Total	395	225

England International Appearances	25
Goals	23

Though he was born in Tyneside, the other Stanley, as he was proud to be known, only had one home – Blackpool. He spent the twilight of his career with other clubs, but never moved home and refused offers to stay in the game, simply because he didn't want to tear up his roots.

He joined the Blackpool groundstaff in 1937 and was nearly rejected for being too slow for the professional game. However, he sharpened up during the war years. His football career was almost cut short in its infancy, when he received severe head and back injuries, when the Wellington bomber he was piloting crashed during the war. For years afterwards, he suffered headaches and sleepless nights, but the fans never knew. Miraculously, he overcame this serious injury to become one of England's finest striking inside-forwards. He was fast moving and possessed fierce shooting ability.

He made his international debut for Wales in wartime against his own country at Wembley on 25th September 1943. Mortensen, then 21, travelled to Wembley as an England reserve but finished up playing for an injury-hit Welsh side when left-half Ivor Powell had to leave the field. England won the war-time international 8-3.

His first full game for England was against Portugal in Lisbon in 1947. It was even more remarkable – England won 10-0 and Mortensen scored four, the first of 23 goals for his country in 25 internationals. In fact, he is one of only four players in this century who have achieved hat-tricks when making their England debuts.

Undoubtedly, his best goal for his country was the first of England's four without reply against Italy in Turin in 1948, when he culminated a scintillating 40-yard run with a curling shot into the roof of the net from a seemingly impossible angle. His final England game was the 6-3 humiliation by the Hungarians at Wembley in 1953, in which he was one of the few home players who were not overwhelmed by the superlative visitors. True to form, he signed off with a goal. He led Blackpool's scorers in each of the six immediate post-war seasons and totalled 197 goals in 317 games for the Bloomfield Road club.

He scored in every round of the 1947-48 F.A. Cup

competition and played in three finals, the best remembered of which will be the 1953 when he notched a hat-trick in his side's 4-3 win over Bolton. Forming a formidable partnership with Stanley Matthews, he brought that same courage as he'd shown after that plane crash to the soccer field. In the Blackpool dressing room, the players had a saying: "Morty's here, never fear."

It was a sad day for Stan in 1955 when the time came for him to leave Blackpool. He signed for Hull City, then went to Southport, before going out of the League with Bath City and Lancaster. He then opened his sports shop close to Bloomfield Road and that was the last football saw of him, apart from a few charity games, until Blackpool called him back to manage them in February 1967 – he was thrilled at the challenge, but unfortunately things didn't work out for him.

A superb opportunist, he will forever be associated with great fightbacks. After leaving football, he became a successful businessman in the town, where he was also a Conservative councillor.

A soccer legend, he died in a Blackpool hospital just four days before his seventieth birthday.

MANCHESTER EVENING NEWS

JACKIE MUDIE

Birthplace:	Dundee
Born:	10th April 1930
Position:	Inside-Forward

Football League Career

	Appearances	Goals
Blackpool	320	143
Stoke City	89	32
Port Vale	54	9
Total	463	184

Scotland International Apperances	17
Goals	9

Born in Dundee, the youngest of six brothers, Jackie Mudie had early ambitions to become a house-painter. Just after his 16th birthday, he joined Blackpool on trial, but within a week had returned to his Dundee home. Fortunately, a change of mind brought him back to Blackpool and he soon established himself as a great prospect. He worked as an apprentice-decorator and at one time, was engaged on painting the Romford Hotel, owned by Stanley Matthews! At the same time, he was playing part-time for Blackpool and sometimes found himself playing alongside seven internationals in the Central League side.

He eventually made the first-team during the 1949-50 season. "He's little but he's wise, a terror for his size" was an apt description of Jackie Mudie going the rounds at that time. He more than atoned for his slight physique by his wonderful ball control, quickness off the mark and ability to snap up scoring chances. He had served with the R.A.F. and was one of their most successful forwards. He gained his first international cap for Scotland against Wales in October 1956, going on to make 17 full appearances. After playing for Blackpool in the 1951 F.A. Cup Final at inside-right, he then established himself at inside-left. In fact, any inside-forward position came the same to Mudie. He was for a long time an admirable partner for the great Stanley Matthews and played at centre-forward for Scotland, notching a hat-trick in a World Cup tie in Switzerland.

Mudie's split-second timing played a big part in many of Blackpool's triumphs. The goal that took the Seasiders to Wembley in 1953 was all down to Mudie. It was against Tottenham Hotspur in the semi-final at Villa Park. In the last minute or so, Alf Ramsey, Spurs' right-back, tried to pass the ball back to goalkeeper Ted Ditchburn. Anticipating the move, Mudie nipped in and before Ditchburn realised the danger, flashed the ball into the net for the winning goal.

Mudie was a credit to both Blackpool and Scotland, but in 1961, he moved to Stoke City, his six goals in the last few matches of the season saving the Potters from relegation to the Third Division. In his second season, he scored 20 goals, Mudie often saying that his years at Stoke were the happiest of his whole career.

In November 1963, he moved on to Port Vale, but throughout his career, he was one of football's sportsmen and gentlemen.

BLACKPOOL EVENING GAZETTE

PHIL NEAL

Birthplace:	Irchester
Born:	29th February 1951
Position:	Full-Back

Football League Career

	Appearances	Goals
Northampton Town	182 (4)	29
Liverpool	453 (2)	41
Bolton Wanderers	58 (8)	3
Total	693 (14)	73

England International Appearances	50
Goals	5

Phil Neal began his League career with Northampton Town after signing professional forms in December 1968. He made his League debut that season, the end of which saw the Cobblers relegated to Division Four. By 1972, he had established himself in the side, playing in a number of positions, but lining up on most occasions as a midfield player. After making 206 first-team appearances for Northampton, he was signed by Bob Paisley for £65,000 in October 1974.

He made his debut for the Reds against Everton the following month as a replacement for the injured Alec Lindsay at left-back. He was an ever-present from his second appearance for the club in December 1974 until missing a defeat against Sunderland in October 1983, a run of 366 consecutive League matches, mostly in the number two shirt.

An intelligent, positional player, he denied the winger any space. Though he was excellent in defence, his distribution was immaculate. The majority of his goals came from the penalty spot, Phil taking this role over from Kevin Keegan in his second season. He hit the clincher in the 1977 Earopean Cup Final from the spot and was on the mark again against A.S. Roma. He played in a total of four European Cup Finals for Liverpool, captaining them in two of them.

His masterly performances at full-back, week in, week out, were an integral part of the Reds' great defensive displays over the years. He was forced to miss the second leg of the European Cup tie against Odense, thus ending a club record of 417 consecutive appearances. He won almost every honour whilst playing for Liverpool, picking up seven Championship medals and was on the winning side in four League Cup Finals. He won a U.E.F.A. Cup winners' medal and four European Cup winners' medals – only an F.A. Cup winners' medal eluded him.

He is the most capped England right-back of all-time with 50 caps to his name. His last appearance for England was against Denmark at Wembley in September 1983.

He succeeded Graeme Souness as skipper for the 1984-85 season, but halfway through the following season, he left to join Bolton Wanderers as player-manager.

He had made 635 first-team appearances for Liverpool and scored 60 goals.

At Bolton, he continued to play, lending his experience to the younger players. His first few years in management were quite eventful. He led the side to Wembley, where they lost 3-0 to Bristol City in the Freight Rover Trophy Final. The club were relegated to the Fourth Division for the first time in their history, but bounced back immediately at the end of the following campaign. There was another visit to Wembley in 1989, Bolton beating Torquay United 4-1 to clinch the Sherpa Van Trophy. All in all, his career tally amounted to 915 League and Cup games and 94 goals, a remarkable tally for a defender who specialised in penalties.

LIVERPOOL DAILY POST & ECHO

KEITH NEWTON

Birthplace:	Manchester
Born:	23rd June 1941
Position:	Full-Back

Football League Career

	Appearances	Goals
Blackburn Rovers	306	9
Everton	48 (1)	1
Burnley	209	5
Total	563 (1)	15

England International Appearances	27
Goals	0

Born in Manchester, Keith Newton started his football career by playing left-back for Didsbury Technical School at the age of 11 and continued to play for them until he was 15. After playing at right-back for Manchester Junior Boys, he played for Spurley Hey Youth Club when he was noticed by Blackburn Rovers.

He signed as a professional in October 1958 and was a member of the successful Blackburn F.A. Youth Cup-winning side of 1959. Having appeared as a centre-half with the youth team, Newton made his first-team debut in the left-half position, but switched to left-back, making the position his own.

Newton was a cultured defender. Tall and athletic, he was sharp in the tackle and sound in the air. He was also noted for his attacking runs down the flank. He finally settled into the right-back spot and won his first major honour in 1964, when he gained the first of several England Under-23 caps against Scotland at Newcastle. Shortly after this, he suffered the first of several major injuries that dogged his career and cost him many representative honours. He injured a knee training with England and had to have a cartilage operation. However, he subsequently made a remarkable recovery in time to go on England's close season Under-23 tour.

He got his first full cap in February 1965 at Wembley against West Germany, but it ended in near disaster. He was carried off the field injured with a suspected broken leg before the interval, but the injury turned out to be less serious than feared. Unfortunately, these injuries hampered his early career and he just missed out on inclusion in the 1966 World Cup. Despite the fact that Rovers were playing in the Second Division, Newton established himself as England's right-back in the late 1960s.

The Blackburn manager tried to persuade Newton that his future lay in midfield and played him there on several occasions. However, Newton was reluctant to switch positions on a permanent basis and reverted to his full-back role.

By 1969, he was a world-rated player, though Rovers were continuing to struggle in Division Two, eventually finishing in the club's lowest ever position.

In December 1969, he joined Everton for £80,000 and helped them to win the 1969-70 League Championship. After the initial success at Everton, Newton became more and more unsettled at the way he was being asked to play and finally lost his place.

In June 1972, he moved to Burnley on a free-transfer, helping them win promotion to the First Division in the 1972-73 season. A cool, cultured and vastly experienced full-back, he remained at Turf Moor for the rest of his League career before finally bowing out at the end of the 1977-78 season.

The following season he had a brief spell in non-League football with Morecambe.

LANCASHIRE EVENING TELEGRAPH

STEVE NICOL

Birthplace:	Irvine
Born:	11th December 1961
Position:	Defender; Midfield

Football League Career

	Appearances	Goals
Liverpool	231 (11)	35
Total	231 (11)	35

Scotland International Appearances	28
Goals	0

As a youngster, Steve Nicol played for Ayr United's Boys' club, where his ability came to the attention of local scouts. He was working as a bricklayer and didn't hesitate when Ayr United offered him professional terms. He made his debut as a centre-half in 1979, before finding a natural niche at left-back. He won the first of his 14 Under-21 caps, a Scottish record, in September 1980 against Sweden.

In October 1981, Glasgow Rangers turned down Ayr's asking price and with 70 games under his belt for the Somerset Park club, he moved south to Liverpool for £300,000.

Consigned to play in the Central League after finding himself up against the consistent Phil Neal, he showed his potential in one of those early reserve games. Picking up the ball in his own penalty area, he beat five opponents as he ran the full length of the field to score the winning goal.

When Joe Fagan took over as manager in 1983, he gave Nicol the chance to prove himself. Craig Johnston was injured and it was Nicol who slotted into his midfield position to play in 19 consecutive matches and earn a Championship medal. At the end of the season, he came on as a substitute in the European Cup Final against A.S. Roma. He volunteered to take Liverpool's first penalty in the shoot-out. He missed, but still went home with a winners' medal.

At the start of the following season, he made his full international debut in Scotland's 6-1 trouncing of Yugoslavia at Hampden Park. For the Reds, he was equally commanding in midfield or at the back. His ability to switch roles and get forward was now an integral part of the Liverpool style. When Phil Neal left to become player-manager at Bolton, he reverted to his principal position of right-back. He was in brilliant form, but a groin injury kept him out for almost two-thirds of the ensuing season.

On his return to the team, he quickly refound his scoring touch, scoring six goals in as many games at the start of Liverpool's march to the 1986-87 League Championship. Over the following seasons, his form was magnificent, both at centre-back in Alan Hansen's absence and more so when playing on the right side of midfield. The right side of midfield is I feel Steve's best position. From there, he has scored some really memorable goals, including a superb chip over the advancing Newcastle 'keeper in September 1987 as he hit a hat-trick. Footballer of the Year in 1989, the versatile Scottish international has played with great distinction in every defensive and midfield position. A reliable stalwart, Nicol's boots are size 12, thus ensuring that he has a better chance than anyone else of getting a toe-end to the ball at crucial moments!

LIVERPOOL DAILY POST & ECHO

ALAN OAKES

Birthplace:	Winsford
Born:	1st September 1942
Position:	Wing-Half

Football League Career

	Appearances	Goals
Manchester City	561 (3)	26
Chester City	211	15
Total	772 (3)	41

Alan Oakes never played any organised football until he left junior school to attend Winsford Secondary Modern. He left school at 15 after representing Mid-Cheshire boys and immediately joined Manchester City. He had always played at inside-forward in school football, but had a number of games at wing-half for the county side and it was this position he adopted when he joined City.

He played his first game for City Reserves in season 1958-59 against Stoke City at Maine Road and made his first-team debut the following season on 14th November 1959 against Chelsea as a stand-in for the injured Ken Barnes. In his debut season, he had to help City fight against relegation which was avoided only in the fortieth match when Colin Barlow's goal secured victory over Preston North End.

It was toward the end of the following season that Ken Barnes retired from the first-class game and Oakes was in! His early years at Maine Road in the first half of the 1960s were spent in a poor City side. However, Oakes held on and was rewarded with plenty of honours in the remainder of his career with City.

He won a Second Division Championship medal, followed by a First Division Championship medal, two League Cup winners' medals, an F.A. Cup winners' medal and a European Cup-Winners' medal.

He didn't manage to acquire a full England cap but he did play for the Football League against the Scottish League at Hampden Park in March 1969. Over the two seasons prior to this he had been chosen for the full England squad on three occasions, but still awaited that elusive first cap. There have certainly been more flamboyant footballers than Alan Oakes who have won England caps, but certainly not as talented. He was a player who made great surging runs from midfield, Young and Coleman in particular benefiting.

Despite playing at wing-half, he was always fortunate enough to score a number of goals for City. Against Athletico Bilbao in the Second Leg of the Cup-Winners' match at Maine Road, after the first leg had been drawn at 3-3, he let fly from fully 30 yards as the Spanish defence backed off and the ball rocketed into the net. Swindon Town were the opponents and when Mike Summerbee (not yet with City) threw the ball to a surprised Oakes, he killed it, swung round and hit it terrifically hard from 40 yards with his left foot to score.

Alan Oakes was a quiet, gentle, unassuming player – a player who got on with the job without any fuss. He was rewarded with a testimonial against Manchester United in 1972. To mark his 500th appearance he was presented with a silver salver before the game against Stoke City on 9th November 1974.

In July 1976, having helped City to yet another success at Wembley, he signed for Chester at a fee of £15,000, later becoming player-manager. His part in the history of Manchester City Football Club cannot be overestimated. He played in 669 games for City – more than any other player.

MANCHESTER EVENING NEWS

STAN PEARSON

STAN PEARSON

Birthplace:	Salford
Born:	11th January 1919
Position:	Inside-Forward

Football League Career

	Appearances	Goals
Manchester United	315	128
Bury	122	56
Chester City	57	16
Total	494	200

England International Appearances	8
Goals	5

Educated at the Frederick Road School, Salford, Stan Pearson joined Manchester United as a professional in May 1936 from the Adelphi Lads' Club which played in the Manchester and District Amateur Football League. He made his League debut for the Reds on 13th November 1937 in a 7-1 win at Chesterfield, at the age of 18. United won promotion at the end of that season, but it wasn't until after the Second World War that he made a big impression on the football scene.

A brainy footballer, he linked superbly with Jack Rowley to form the most dangerous of strike forces. He hit the first of his five hat-tricks for United in September 1946 as they beat Liverpool 5-0 at Old Trafford. His second came in the last match of the following season, as United beat Blackburn 4-1. He was a consistent scorer, with 1951-52 being his last season, as he scored 22 goals in 41 games. He could spray out some marvellous sweeping passes and was equally good enough to get on the end of the resultant crosses.

When United won the F.A. Cup in 1948, Stan Pearson played a leading role. There were one or two scares along the way for the Reds, the first being in the Third Round tie at Villa Park. Aston Villa scored almost from kick-off, but United gave Villa a footballing lesson, going in at half-time 5-1 ahead. The second half produced a tremendous battle with Villa pulling it back to 5-4. There were certainly signs of panic in the United defence, but Stan Pearson chipped in with a late goal which knocked the heart out of the Midlands side. That proved United's toughest confrontation on the road to Wembley – even Derby County in the semi-final didn't give as much trouble. County scored, but a magic hat-trick by Pearson took United to Wembley, where he added another in United's 4-2 win over Blackpool. He represented the Football League and won eight full England caps.

He appeared in almost 350 games for Manchester United and scored 149 goals. With Matt Busby's youth policy beginning to bring great success, he ended his 17-year career with the club and signed for Bury in February 1954.

At Gigg Lane, he played 122 League games, scoring 56 goals before moving on to Chester in October 1957, eventually succeeding John Harris as manager. That was in May 1959, but two and a half years later, he resigned and took over a newsagent's business in Prestbury, coaching and managing the East Cheshire League side at the same time.

A stylish footballer of immense power, Stan Pearson had the ability to score goals as well as create them.

MANCHESTER EVENING NEWS

FRED PICKERING

Birthplace:	Blackburn
Born:	19th January 1941
Position:	Centre-Forward

Football League Career

	Appearances	Goals
Blackburn Rovers	134	61
Everton	97	56
Birmingham City	74	27
Blackpool	48 (1)	24
Total	353 (1)	168

England International Appearances	3
Goals	5

When he turned professional with Blackburn Rovers in 1958, Fred Pickering was being groomed as a full-back, but with the club so well served in that department his opportunities were limited. He had enjoyed success in the Rovers' junior teams, helping to win the F.A. Youth Cup in 1959, but when given a first-team chance, he had failed to make a lasting impression.

Rovers' manager Jack Marshall decided to gamble with him at centre-forward after some powerful displays in that position whilst playing with the Reserves. Despite his initial clumsy approach work, Pickering had the happy knack of putting the ball in the net and was soon to make quite a name for himself. He had begun to add pace and power to his game and played havoc with the best defences in the land.

After 123 League games and 59 goals in the Blackburn first team, he became unsettled and wanted a transfer. Blackburn were in their best League position for years, but incredibly and controversially, the club let him go.

A fee of £85,000 took him to Everton, where he was, at the time, the highest-priced player in a domestic transfer deal. It was to prove a wise signing, as the tall, dashing centre-forward threatened defences throughout the First Division.

He began well by scoring a hat-trick on his home debut, yet it was in those final few games of the season that Everton lost the title – Pickering possibly upsetting the balance and rhythm of the side! He still netted nine goals in nine matches. Fred Pickering is one of only four players this century who have achieved hat-tricks when making their debuts for England in full internationals – this he achieved against the U.S.A. in May 1964. In 1964-65, he proved to be worth every penny of his huge transfer fee as he collected 27 goals. In March 1966 in the local derby with Liverpool, he was completely on his own when he twisted and his leg collapsed under him. After missing a couple of games, he returned only for it to go again against Sheffield United, when he went up for a high ball and came down on his knee. He had to miss the F.A. Cup semi-final, and the Final against Sheffield Wednesday.

Popular with the Everton fans, he could, with fewer injuries and a different temperament, have become one of the really great Everton footballers.

In August 1967, he moved to Birmingham City for £50,000 and proved to be a prolific marksman for the Midlands club with 27 goals in 74 League appearances.

He returned to Lancashire in 1969 when Blackpool paid £45,000 for him. After helping the Seasiders to win promotion to the First Division, he returned to Blackburn in March 1971. Pickering was cast in the role of a saviour as Rovers faced Third Division football for the first time in their history. Early in 1971-72, Rovers' boss Ken Furphy allowed him to be released, claiming he was out of condition. He attempted to revive his career with Brighton, but without success. Though he made his mark with Everton, he will always be remembered to Blackburn fans as the player who could have led the club to Championship success.

LANCASHIRE EVENING TELEGRAPH

KEVIN RATCLIFFE

Birthplace:	Deeside
Born:	12th November 1960
Position:	Defender

Football League Career

	Appearances	Goals
Everton	349 (1)	2
Total	349 (1)	2

Wales International Appearances	52
Goals	0

Kevin Ratcliffe was born in Mancot and played in the same Flintshire schools side as Ian Rush. On completion of his education, a host of top sides offered Ratcliffe apprentice forms, but there was only one club that interested him and he duly signed on for his beloved Everton. For on the rare occasions he was not kicking a ball about as a boy, he could be found cheering on the likes of Ball and Royle from the Goodison terraces.

He signed professional forms in 1978, but after kicking his heels in the Reserves for two years, he made his League debut against Manchester United in March 1980. He played in one other game that season, but did enough to earn both an Under-21 call up and a first-team place by the start of 1980-81. In November 1980, he made his full international debut for Wales against Czechoslovakia, marking dangerman Masny out of the game. When Howard Kendall took over as Everton manager in May 1981, he played Ratcliffe at centre-back and appointed him captain. Since then, he has become the calming influence in both the Everton and Wales teams. His role at Everton is crucial as the Blues game is built on a very sound defensive system. They often play a tight and rigid offside game, but if a striker does break through, Ratcliffe's speed is such that the danger is snuffed out immediately. Strong in the tackle, Ratcliffe possesses quite a ruthless streak that means he can't be intimidated!

Under his inspired leadership, Everton marched to two League Championship successes in 1985 and 1987. He lifted the F.A. Cup in 1984 after Everton's 2-0 win over Watford and the European Cup Winners' Cup in 1985 after a 3-1 win over Rapid Vienna.

The then manager of Wales, Mike England, enthused over Ratcliffe's influence and made him captain. In April 1987, he reached another professional milestone in captaining Wales against Czechoslovakia – his fortieth international cap, so beating Everton's previous club record of 39 caps, set by England's Alan Ball.

He now seems to have recovered fully from the serious groin injury which has plagued him over the past few seasons. Despite losing some of his astonishing speed, he still retains the style and consistency that have made him one of the world's classiest central defenders.

LIVERPOOL DAILY POST & ECHO

PETER REID

Birthplace: Huyton
Born: 20th May 1956
Position: Midfield

Football League Career

	Appearances	Goals
Bolton Wanderers	222 (3)	23
Everton	157 (2)	8
Queen's Park Rangers	29	1
Manchester City	46 (4)	1
Total	454 (9)	33

England International Appearances	13
Goals	0

Born and bred on Merseyside, Peter Reid played schoolboy football for Huyton Boys. It was a successful side and caused something of an upset when they won the English Schools Trophy in 1970. Many scouts came to the games and the chance came for Reid to join various clubs as an apprentice. He opted for Bolton and made his debut as a substitute at home to Orient in October 1974.

Reid soon established himself in the Bolton side and was ever-present for the next two seasons – when Bolton just missed out on promotion. His cultured midfield play and his intense desire to be involved all the time were features of Bolton's Second Division championship winning side of 1977-78. This season also saw him appear for the England Under-21 side. Injury struck in a pre-season game and Reid missed Bolton's return to the top flight. He recovered to win back his midfield spot, but again suffered the misfortune of a broken leg. On New Year's Day 1979, he collided with Everton goalkeeper George Wood on a snowbound Burnden Park pitch, the game later being abandoned. This time Reid was missing for a year, his return coming too late to save the Wanderers from relegation in 1980.

Contractual problems prevented Reid from playing after he failed to agree terms with Arsenal, Wolves and Everton, all of whom offered £600,000 for his signature. Eventually, he was placed on a weekly contract, but in September 1981, he broke his leg again in a 3-0 defeat at Barnsley. The midfield star again won his battle for fitness, realising his ambition to get back into the top flight when he signed for Everton.

It proved to be one of Everton's most significant post-war signings. With Bolton, he showed that he possessed a rare combination of talents, a ball-winner and creator who could also poach goals. He wasn't an immediate success at Everton, playing just seven League games from the New Year.

At the end of the 1984-85 season, Peter Reid was chosen by the Professional Footballers' Association as their player of the year. This came a season after he had won one of the Rothman Football Awards. The Rothman Annual that year stated: “A few years ago, injury and disputes seemed to have ruined the first-class career of this midfield player. During a spell of five years at Burnden Park, he failed to make a score of appear-ances in any one season for Bolton Wanderers.” Reid was the inspiration behind Everton’s revival, powerfully initiating attacks while blocking and threatening the skills of the opposition. At Goodison Park, he won two League Championship medals, an F.A. Cup winners’ medal and a European Cup-winners’ medal, along with 13 England caps, the first as substitute against Mexico in 1985. In 1987-88, he was appointed player-coach at Everton before being transferred to Queen’s Park Rangers in 1989. After a short stay at Loftus Road, he returned to the north-west, joining Manchester City in December 1989. After Howard Kendall returned to Everton, Reid was the players’ and supporters’ choice to replace him. City finished last season in fifth place, their highest League position since 1978.

MANCHESTER EVENING NEWS

BRYAN ROBSON

Birthplace: Chester-le-Street
Born: 11th January 1957
Position: Midfield

Football League Career

	Appearances	Goals
West Bromwich Albion	194 (4)	39
Manchester United	284 (4)	68
Total	478 (8)	107

England International Appearances 90
Goals 26

Bryan Robson's original football home is the north-east where, as a teenager, he would stand on the terraces of St James' Park, Newcastle and shout on the Magpies. He couldn't get into the Durham School's team as a youngster at just 5ft 2ins and 7 stone at the time.

He joined West Bromwich Albion in 1974 and they attempted to build him up in both physique and stature. His landlady would send him out at the start of the day with a mixture of raw egg, milk, sherry and sugar, followed by a nightcap of a bottle of Mackeson!

At the Hawthorns, he played in several positions, this helping him to understand many new things about the game. He best expressed his skills in midfield, where he provided the ideal service for Regis and Cunningham. He suffered a great setback in the 1976-77 season when he broke a leg three times. However, determination kept bringing him back and when Albion boss, Ron Atkinson took charge at Manchester United, he returned to the Hawthorns and took Robson to Old Trafford.

Manchester United broke the transfer record when they paid West Brom £1.5 million for Bryan Robson – hardly surprising that they made the signing into a public ceremony out on the Old Trafford pitch. His United League debut came in the following game against Manchester City at Maine Road – Robson having a sound game in a goalless draw.

The following season, he reached two Cup Finals at Wembley with the Reds – his move had been justified.

Initially a back four player, he developed the attacking side of his game to such an extent, that his powerful surges from midfield into the penalty area have become his trademark. His midfield brilliance earned him a place in England's 1982 World Cup squad. He scored England's first goal in their opening game against France in a record 27 seconds.

Bryan Robson takes into the international game all the physical aggression needed to withstand the pressures of the English Football League, yet he also has a natural class that would impress in any of the World XI's of the past. He shows great versatility on the field of play – strong and precise in defensive tackles, working as hard as two men in midfield and possessing great stamina that allows him to get into goalscoring positions.

It is perhaps as captain that Robson has made his greatest impression, both for Manchester United and England. He has led United to F.A. Cup Final victories and was the two-goal hero of the 1983 4-0 replay win over Brighton.

In 1986, Manchester United refused Robson permission to undergo surgery after he dislocated a shoulder, when he ran into the electricity box controlling Old Trafford's undersoil heating, as he typically went full pelt after a centre. It continued to let him down as United kept playing in a vain attempt to claim the Championship. He found himself torn between club and country, for England wanted him fully fit for the 1986 World Cup finals in Mexico.

He was the only England player to show his true form in the 1988 European Championships – though England's three consecutive defeats were a great disappointment to him.

Last season he led United to victory over Barcelona in Rotterdam as the Reds deservedly lifted the European Cup-Winners' Cup.

MANCHESTER EVENING NEWS

Despite an injury-hit career, that includes four broken legs, three dislocated shoulders, torn ankle ligaments, broken nose and concussion, he is one of the truly great footballers of the present day.

JACK ROWLEY

Birthplace:	Wolverhampton
Born:	7th October 1920
Position:	Forward

Football League Career

	Appearances	Goals
Bournemouth	11	10
Manchester United	380	182
Plymouth Argyle	56	14
Total	447	206

England International Appearances	6
Goals	6

Jack Rowley was born in Wolverhampton to a footballing family. His father was a goalkeeper for Walsall, who even played for a local team when he was nearly 60. Jack started out as an outside-left, becoming part of Major Frank Buckley's famous nursery at Wolves as a groundstaff boy. However, Wolves didn't rate him too highly and he was allowed to join Bournemouth. After 11 games and 10 goals for the Dean Court side, United signed him for £3,000, Rowley playing his first game against Sheffield Wednesday at Old Trafford in October 1937. Needing time to settle into his new surroundings, he asked to play in the reserves. A few weeks later, he returned to first-team action and scored four goals as United beat Swansea 5-1.

During the wartime, he guested for Spurs, Wolves and Irish club Distillery. He played for Spurs one week and scored seven goals and then a few days later got eight out of eight for Wolves!

Dubbed 'The Gunner' because his shot was reckoned to be the hardest of his day, his style was both strong and aggressive.

He dominated United's scoring in the early post-war years, especially on the big occasions – he hit two in the 1948 F.A. Cup Final victory over Blackpool. He started the 1951-52 season in fine style, scoring a hat-trick in each of the first two games. Indeed, after only seven games he had rattled in an incredible 14 goals.

He scored goals right to the end of his career with United. His last game was on January 22nd 1955 in a 1-1 draw with Bolton Wanderers at Old Trafford. He appeared in 422 League and Cup games for United, scoring 208 goals. His first division tally alone was 182 goals in 380 games, including 30 in 40 Championship-winning fixtures in 1951-52 – a United record until it was broken by Dennis Viollet in 1960.

After 18 years with United, he was granted a free transfer and joined Plymouth Argyle as a player-manager. He took the Pilgrims into the Second Division in 1959 before his next job at Boundary Park, where he took Oldham up to the Third Division. After an unbelievable cloak and dagger campaign, he was sacked and went to Holland, succeeding Vic Buckingham as manager of Ajax Amsterdam. After leading the Dutch side to the runners-up spot, his contract wasn't renewed. He returned to these shores for spells with Wrexham, Bradford and Oldham again.

On retiring from football, he took a sub-post office at Shaw near Oldham. Jack was the brother of that brilliant goalscorer Arthur. Amazingly, they both scored their 200th League goal on the same day – October 22nd 1955. It was Jack who reached the milestone first by just 12 minutes!

MANCHESTER EVENING NEWS

JOE ROYLE

Birthplace:	Liverpool
Born:	8th April 1949
Position:	Centre-Forward

Football League Career

	Appearances	Goals
Everton	229 (3)	102
Manchester City	98 (1)	23
Bristol	100 (1)	18
Norwich City	40 (2)	9
Total	477 (7)	152

England International Appearances	6
Goals	2

Even though he was brought up within a stone's throw of the Everton Ground, Joe Royle used to watch Manchester United as much as possible!

If Joe had followed his father's trade, he would have entertained crowds in a far different way, for Joe's father was a musician with a local trio.

He made his debut for Everton against Blackpool in January 1966 at the tender age of 16, thus becoming the youngest-ever player to represent this club. He came in for Alex Young and even at that age, he was stocky and powerful and had all the energy, confidence and skill of youth. It was after this game – Everton were beaten 2-0 – that manager Harry Catterick was attacked by the fans. Young Joe made only one more first-team appearance that season at Leeds and Everton were beaten again, this time 4-1.

The 1966-67 season was almost ended before Joe Royle was again given his chance. He grabbed it – hitting two goals in a 3-1 win over Chelsea at Goodision. That was the first time Joe had appeared before his own fans for the League side. It was a display that banished the bitter Blackpool memory. He played in four games towards the end of that campaign, netting three goals.

They didn't come much bigger than Royle, standing an inch over six feet and tipping the scales at around 13st 4lbs. Within four years, he had packed a wealth of experience into his sizeable frame and earned himself the reputation as one of Everton's finest post-war strikers and a fitting successor to the traditions of Dixie Dean and Tommy Lawton.

In 1967-68, Joe's first ever Cup goal saw Everton narrowly beat then Third Division Southport 1-0 in the F.A. Cup Third Round. He was a centre-forward with honest-to-goodness ideas about what his job demanded – the scoring of goals!

He was the Blues' leading marksman in the 1968-69 season with 22 goals and again the following season with 23 goals as Everton won the Championship. He was one of the deadliest strikers of a ball in the First Division. He was powerful with a clinical finish and an ability to head the ball not seen at Goodison since the days of Dixie Dean. His career had been dogged by injury and he eventually moved to Manchester City. It was a little suprising that Everton boss Billy Bingham should let him go at the time he did, for the Blues were desperately short of goalscoring talent.

He was one of the most prolific goalscorers since the war, scoring 119 goals in 272 games for Everton.

He won six international caps, the first coming against Malta in 1971.

He played in one League match short of a hundred for Manchester City, before moving on to Bristol City and later Norwich. Entering management with Oldham Athletic, he has been a revelation, the Latics finally winning the Second Division championship title this last season when Neil Redfearn's injury-time penalty gave them a 3-2 win over Sheffield Wednesday in the last game of the season. A man who talks eagerly about the game and the people in it, he still appears to be placid and easy-going!

MANCHESTER EVENING NEWS

IAN RUSH

Birthplace: St Asaph
Born: 20th October 1961
Position: Striker

Football League Career

	Appearances	Goals
Chester City	33 (1)	14
Liverpool	313 (8)	179
Total	346 (9)	193

Wales International Appearances	48
Goals	18

A schoolboy international from the tiny Welsh village of St Asaph, he started his career with Chester. After just 34 League appearances, which had yielded 14 goals, Bob Paisley paid £300,000 for the youngster. Many doubted the shrewdness of this acquisition and in his early days at Anfield, he could hardly find the net in Central League games -there was even talk of him moving on. Liverpool took care not to rush Rush. He became a full international over six months before his first-team debut, first as a substitute in the 0-1 defeat by Scotland on 21st May 1980, then as a full cap against Northern Ireland at Cardiff. His first goal for Wales came in May 1982 against the Irish at Wrexham. By this time, he had been blooded at Anfield and become a firm favourite of the Kop.

In the 1981-82 season, he scored 30 goals in 49 games, to win his first League Championship medal. There were further League titles in 1983 and 1984, European Cup victory in 1984 and League Cup wins in 1983 and 1984. The derby game with Everton in 1982-83 saw Liverpool rout the Blues at Goodison 5-0 with Rush netting four. His impact on the F.A. Cup competition was immediate, scoring on his debut for Chester in their 5-1 drubbing of Workington in the first round in November 1979. He scored two F.A. Cup hat-tricks, in March 1985 when Liverpool beat Barnsley 4-0 at Oakwell and then in 1989 when Liverpool thrashed Swansea City 8-0 at Anfield.
In 1983-84, Ian Rush won the Golden Boot Award with his 32 goals scored in Division One matches.
Unlike some run-of-the-mill strikers Ian Rush is the focal point of the Liverpool attacks, collecting the ball out of defence and laying it off simply but effectively before speeding off to a new position. The sight of him breaking free to leave defenders in his wake before slotting home the ball, is one that will linger long in the memory.
Perhaps the peak of his career was 1986, when the Reds lifted the near-impossible League and Cup double, with Rush scoring twice in the 3-1 F.A. Cup Final victory over Everton.
Ian Rush deeply appreciated being voted Player of the Year in 1984. Liverpool's dependence on Rush's flow of goals was shown by the run of 144 matches in which the side never lost when Ian scored. That record was broken

when his 202nd goal was overtaken by two from Charlie Nicholas as Arsenal won the 1987 Littlewood's Cup.

Rush's reputation as one of the world's most feared strikers had clubs battling for his signature. Juventus succeeded in a deal worth £3.2 million. There was one consolation for the Anfield faithful in that he would be staying for one more season. Rush showed his greatness by playing his heart out and scoring 30 goals in 42 League games. He ended the season in style, hitting two goals in a 3-1 win over Everton, bringing his tally in derby matches to 19, equalling Dixie Dean's record. He hit the winner in the final game at Anfield against Watford, before throwing his shirt to the Kop. When Rush left for Italy in 1987, he had overtaken Dalglish's club record of 116 League goals and reached a total of 207 in all competitions. This, spread over 330 appearances, was a great achievement against tightly-packed defences.

Following an unhappy time in Italy, Rush returned to the Anfield fold in a sensational £2.8 million transfer just before the start of the 1988-89 season. Coming on as substitute in the 1989 FA Cup final against Everton, Rush scored two goals as Liverpool won 3-2 after extra-time, taking his total of derby goals to 21 to pass Dixie Dean's record of long ago.

A goalscoring phenomenon, he has scored at the rate of 4 goals every 7 matches – quite an extraordinary record in the modern game. His record is the more remarkable, for so many of his goals have come in top matches, with trophies at stake.

LIVERPOOL DAILY POST & ECHO

IAN ST JOHN

Birthplace:	Motherwell
Born:	7th June 1938
Position:	Midfield; Forward

Football League Career

	Appearances	Goals
Liverpool	334 (2)	95
Coventry City	18	3
Tranmere Rovers	9	1
Total	361 (2)	99

Scotland International Appearances	21
Goals	9

After paying Motherwell £37,500 for the Scottish international forward, Bill Shankly described Ian St John as the man the Reds couldn't afford not to buy, the most urgently needed component of his new team.

His first appearance in a red shirt was in a Liverpool Senior Cup Final against Everton at Goodison Park in August 1961 – he was an instant hit with the fans, as he scored a hat-trick!

St John was strong, courageous and quite devastating in the air for a man of 5ft 7$^{1}/_{2}$ins. His delicate flicks did much to promote a fine understanding with Roger Hunt – he scored 18 goals that first season as the Reds won promotion. During that Division Two title campaign, he often showed flashes of bad temper and in March 1962, he was sent off along with Preston's Tony Singleton after such a clash – however, fire was certainly an integral part of 'The Saint's' make-up.

His first season in the top flight saw him score 19 goals and then 21 in 1963-64 as Liverpool went on to win the Championship. During that successful campaign, Jimmy Melia, Liverpool's scheming inside-forward was injured and Shanks withdrew St John into a deep-lying role. He showed his true potential and became the mastermind of the Reds' attack. He gave his team-mates plenty of possession and created space for them with his intelligent running.

It certainly wasn't the end of his goals, his jack-knife header against Leeds at Wembley in 1965 winning the F.A. Cup.

Roger Hunt would be the first to admit that he benefited greatly from St John's talents as he readily acknowledged after the 1965 European Cup Winners' Cup tie against Belgian side Standard Liege.

After running half the length of the field, drawing defenders with him, he slipped the ball through to an unmarked Hunt to score.

As his fitness began to decline, he was used a little more sparingly. On the substitutes' bench for the European Fairs Cup tie against Dynamo Bucharest, he was brought into the game with Liverpool holding a precarious 1-0 lead. With his touch and close passing skills, he laid on two goals near the end of the match to leave the Reds comfortable winners at 3-0.

'The Saint' was a tough and tenacious player, representing Scotland on 21 occasions. On leaving Anfield, he had short spells with Coventry City and Tranmere, before trying coaching and then management. He didn't succeed as many people thought he might and eventually he became a TV personality. He now shares the screen with another great goalscorer from the 1960s, Jimmy Greaves.

In the years to come, it is not as Greavsie's chat show partner that he should be recalled, but as the first piece of the Liverpool jigsaw that has had success over the last three decades.

WALLY & HOWARD TALBOT PHOTOGRAPHY

KEVIN SHEEDY

Birthplace:	Builth Wells
Born:	21st October 1959
Position:	Midfield

Football League Career

	Appearances	Goals
Hereford United	47 (4)	4
Liverpool	1 (2)	0
Everton	252 (7)	66
Total	300 (13)	70

Republic of Ireland International Appearances	34
Goals	6

Born and bred in North Wales, Kevin Sheedy was delighted when on leaving school, he was offered apprentice terms by Third Division Hereford United. Making his League debut against Preston North End in April 1976, he went on to make 51 League appearances before an £80,000 move to Liverpool in July 1978.

However, things didn't work out for the young midfielder. In four years at Anfield, he made just three League appearances for the Reds. He won four Central League Championship medals before in June 1982, he was rescued from obscurity when Everton manager Howard Kendall paid £100,000 for his services. Sheedy was anxious to move to a club where he could be assured of first-team football. He scored his first goal for the club in a 3-1 home win over Spurs.

He made his internationald debut in October 1983 as a substitute in the game against Holland. Despite being born in North Wales, he had qualified to play for the Republic of Ireland through his father. His appearances were limited by injury, as they were for Everton. He had no problem in securing himself a regular first-team spot, yet he was still dogged by misfortune. He missed Everton's 2-0 win over Watford in the 1984 F.A. Cup Final through injury, thus missing a winners' medal.

He was back for the following season, playing a vital role as Everton lifted the League Championship for the first time in 15 years. In May of that Championship-winning season, he scored the third goal in the European Cup-Winners' Cup Final victory over Rapid Vienna. Sheedy has earned himself a reputation as one of the most dangerous free-kick specialists in the game today.

He has scored some goals of superb quality – against Ipswich at Goodison in the sixth round of the F.A. Cup, he scored twice from the same free kick. He bent the first attempt over the wall and into the roof of the net on Paul Cooper's right, but the referee hadn't blown for it to be taken. When the kick was re-taken, he bent it over the wall again to Cooper's left!

In 1987, he was fully fit and helped Everton to win another Championship title. The following year he was instrumental in his adopted country reaching the

LIVERPOOL DAILY POST & ECHO

European Championship Finals.
At the end of the 1987-88 season, he came to the end of his contract at Everton. Top clubs from home and abroad were queuing up for his signature, but to the relief of the Everton fans, manager Harvey persuaded him to sign a new four-and-a-half year deal.

TOMMY SMITH

Birthplace:	Liverpool
Born:	5th April 1945
Position:	Wing-half; Defence

Football League Career

	Appearances	Goals
Liverpool	467 (2)	36
Swansea City	34 (2)	2
Total	501 (2)	38

England International Appearances	1
Goals	0

Born within a corner kick's distance of Anfield, Tommy Smith grew up to become one of the club's greatest servants. He developed into one of the toughest defenders in the Football League and was for a while club captain. He signed professional forms for Liverpool in April 1962 and made his debut at home to Birmingham City in May 1963, standing in for the injured Gordon Milne at right-half. In his Reserve days at Anfield, it was rumoured that he was a target for Manchester United but nothing came of it.

Tommy Smith became an integral member of Bill Shankly's first great Liverpool side. He had two roles, initially in midfield before moving into the centre of defence. His game boasted more skill than it was given credit for and Smith contributed greatly to Liverpool's F.A. Cup success of 1965 and the ensuing Championship campaign.

When he moved into defence, Bill Shankly told him: "Think of yourself as Ron Yeats' right leg" and he developed into a player of great authority. He was the obvious choice to succeed the big Scotsman as captain, which he did in March 1970.

As leader, Smith was an inspiration, driving the team on to greater efforts. He relished the position and its responsibilities and in the 1970-71 season gave some of his best ever performances. He won his only England cap and was only just pipped as Footballer of the Year by Arsenal's Frank McLintock. He led Liverpool to the F.A. Cup Final in 1971, when they lost to Arsenal, before leading the Reds to a unique double of League Championship and U.E.F.A. Cup in 1972-73. After being dropped in November 1973, he had heated words with Bill Shankly; this confrontation losing Smith the captaincy to Emlyn Hughes. He almost moved to Stoke City, but returned to the side to replace the injured Chris Lawler at right-back. After winning more trophies and troubled by knee problems, he announced his retirement in early 1977.

However, Phil Thompson was injured and he found himself back in the centre of defence. He had a superb season, facing Manchester United at Wembley in the F.A. Cup Final, winning another League Championship medal and then making his 600th appearance in a Liverpool shirt in the European Final against Borussia Moenchengladbach. The veteran of so many past glories, he rose majestically to meet Heighway's corner to send a header of immense power crashing into the Germans' net. He stayed for another season and would probably have played against Bruges in the European Cup Final but dropped a pick-axe on his foot!

Though he was offered a one-year contract, he joined John Toshack at Swansea, after he'd made him a better offer. He later made a brief Anfield return as coach.

A player of great courage, toughness and determination, he will go down in folklore as one of the hardest men the game has known.

For his services to the game Tommy Smith was awarded the M.B.E. in 1976.

LIVERPOOL DAILY POST & ECHO

GRAEME SOUNESS

Birthplace:	Edinburgh	
Born:	6th May 1953	
Position:	Midfield	

Football League Career

	Appearances	Goals
Middlesbrough	174 (2)	22
Liverpool	246 (1)	38
Total	420 (3)	60

Scotland International Appearances	54
Goals	3

Though he was born in Edinburgh, Graeme Souness began his career at White Hart Lane, where he was regarded as a 'Fancy Dan' type of player, enjoying life to the full off the field and full of tricks on it, but lacking professionalism.

Souness was on Tottenham's books for three years but never played for them in a senior game, although he figured in the successful Youth Cup team of the early 1970s.

He showed his own head-strong quality when he left Spurs to join Middlesbrough in pursuit of first-team football.

At Ayresome Park, he came under the influence of Jack Charlton, the straight-forward Geordie giving Souness a new, more professional approach to the game, although he retained his enjoyment of the good things enough to keep his nickname of 'Champagne Charlie'.

It was Bob Paisley who brought Souness to Anfield in January 1978 for £352,000 – then a record deal between Football League clubs. Making his debut against West Bromwich Albion, he didn't put a foot wrong as he hinted at the times to come.

His move to Liverpool to team up with Kenny Dalglish was the foundation stone of the club's success over the next decade. The two dove-tailed perfectly, as Souness provided the pass for Dalglish to score the winning-goal against Bruges in the 1978 European Cup Final. There were occasions when his tackling evoked resentment from opponents, but he was to stamp his influence on crucial matches for both Liverpool and Scotland. His displays in the European Cup campaign of 1980-81 were eye-catching, with his sense of awareness and great ability to rip open the hearts of defences with long, telling passes. He also hit two hat-tricks in the early stages of the competition as Liverpool beat Finland's Champions Oulo Palloseura 10-1 and C.S.K.A. Sofia of Bulgaria 5-1 in the Anfield legs.

In March 1982, Spurs felt the full force as he came on as substitute (the only time he was in his time at Anfield) with the Reds two goals down. He was returning after a back injury and helped pull the game round, the final score being 2-2. He scored some valuable goals for

LIVERPOOL DAILY POST & ECHO

Liverpool, none perhaps more valuable than the goal which beat Everton in the 1984 Milk Cup Final replay.

Replacing Phil Thompson as captain, he led the Reds to three successive League titles and League/Milk Cups and one European Cup, thus becoming the most successful skipper in the club's history. In June 1984, he moved to Sampdoria in Italy for £650,000. Two quiet seasons were followed by his surprise appointment as player-manager at Ibrox in 1986.

In his first game he was sent off! The club's disciplinary record has been far from good and three players were sent off this last season in the match against rivals Celtic, but Souness bought wisely in the shape of Terry Butcher and Chris Woods and Rangers won the Championship in his first season.

As a footballer, he was one of the few British players of the 1980s to merit world-class status. With tremendous stamina allied to a great abundance of skill and a true footballing brain, Souness personified the true spirit of the Liverpool midfield department. Souness' no-nonsense approach as a player is matched only by his desire to win as a manager; so it came as no real surprise when he returned to Anfield towards the end of last season as the new supremo.

NEVILLE SOUTHALL

Birthplace:	Llandudno
Born:	16th September 1958
Position:	Goalkeeper

Football League Career

	Appearances	Goals
Bury	39	0
Port Vale (on loan)	9	0
Everton	329	0
Total	377	0

Wales International Appearances	48
Goals	0

As a boy, Neville Southall played for the Caernarvon District side as a centre-half, but after limited success, he shelved any thoughts about being an outfield player to concentrate on goalkeeping. He spent the six years between leaving school and becoming a full-time footballer, working as a dustman, a mopper-up in a cafe and a hod carrier on a building site.

While living in Llandudno, he played for both Bangor City and Conwy United, but it was his fine form at Winsford United that caused Bury to pay £6,000 for him in 1980.

In July 1981 and after only 44 first-team appearances for the Shakers, he signed for Everton in a £150,000 deal. He made his debut for the Blues on 17th October 1981 in a 2-1 win over Ipswich. Things didn't go too smoothly for him after that, for after a 5-0 home defeat against Liverpool, Southall was dropped and sent on loan to Fourth Division Port Vale in January 1983. He returned to Goodison Park after nine games and was ever-present for that and the next two seasons, as his form and Everton's improved beyond all expectations.

He had made his international debut on 27th May 1982, keeping a clean sheet as Wales beat Northern Ireland 3-0. Along with Arsenal's Jack Kelsey, he is the finest goalkeeper to have represented the Welsh.

At 6ft 1ins and weighing in at 12 stone, he had the ideal physique for a goalkeeper. His anticipation is superb and he is a good shot-stopper. Always displaying great courage, he is not afraid to dive in amid a mass of boots to take low crosses.

In 1984, he got his first taste of glory when Everton won the F.A. Cup for the first time in 18 years, beating Watford 2-0. The following season, Everton won the League, the European Cup Winners' Cup and were runners-up in the F.A. Cup. At the end of the season, he became the fourth goalkeeper to win the Player of the Year award, following in the footsteps of Bert Trautmann, Gordon Banks and Pat Jennings – his years of hard work and dedication had paid off.

He suffered severe dislocation of the ankle and ligament damage playing for Wales against the Republic of Ireland in March 1986. The injury was so acute, that it was wondered if he would ever be able to get back to his brilliant best. He recovered in time to collect his second League winners' medal as Everton won the Championship again in 1987. His world-class performances have played a major part in Everton's rise to one of England's top clubs. He possesses brilliant reflexes, which have enabled him to make some outstanding saves.

As his Welsh team-mate and Liverpool number nine Ian Rush says: "For sheer consistency, there's no-one to touch Neville."

LIVERPOOL DAILY POST & ECHO

NOBBY STILES

Birthplace: Manchester
Born: 18th May 1942
Position: Wing-Half

Football League Career

	Appearances	Goals
Manchester United	312	18
Middlesbrough	57	2
Preston North End	44 (2)	1
Total	413 (2)	21

England International Appearances	28
Goals	3

Hailing from Collyhurst (Manchester's most productive football area) he won five England schoolboy caps before signing for the Reds as an apprentice in 1957. Turning professional in 1959, he made his League debut in October 1960 at the age of 18 in a 1-1 draw at Burnden Park and stayed in the side for the remainder of the season.

He shared in United's successful 1963 F.A. Cup run, though he didn't win a place in the Final. He hardly missed a match in 1966-67 when the Reds won the League Championship.

He wore the Number 4 shirt throughout England's triumphant World Cup in 1966. He made his mark as a world-class player with his brilliant covering, especially against Portugal's Eusebio in the semi-final. No one will forget Nobby's antics after England had won the World Cup. He put the trophy on his head and danced with delight.

It has been said that many of Nobby's awkward-looking tackles in the early days were probably because he wasn't wearing his spectacles and that his tackling only improved after he was fitted with contact lenses! After United won the European Cup in 1968, Nobby's standing in the game was at a peak, but his earlier bad boy image was reflected by his pen picture in the match programme when the Reds played Estudiantes in the World Club Championship; he was described as "brutal, badly intentioned and a bad sportsman."

The fans abroad certainly didn't like Nobby, for in his time, he was called an assassin in South America, spat at in Italy and hit on the head by a bottle in Madrid! Playing without his false teeth made him look like Dracula and according to the French, who met him in the 1966 World Cup tournament, he was twice as dangerous!

Although only 1.65m tall and weighing less than 68kg, Nobby Stiles had a reputation for fierce tackling. His tigerish play as a wing-half earned him the respect of team-mates and opponents. Small he may have been in stature, but his heart was as big as his frame. Known to his team-mates as 'Happy', he worked hard for the team, his enthusiasm rubbing off on to other people.

At the age of 27, he suffered two cartilage operations and

in May 1971, United accepted a £20,000 offer from Middlesbrough. He had played first-team football at Old Trafford for 11 seasons, making 393 appearances. After two seasons at Ayresome Park, he moved to Deepdale for the same fee to play for Bobby Charlton. He only played for one more season, but then spent a further seven years there, three as coach and the last four as manager. In 1979-80, he won a Bell's Whisky Manager of the Month Award.

On leaving North End, he teamed up with his brother-in-law Johnny Giles, Nobby becoming coach at Vancouver Whitecaps.

He followed Johnny to the Hawthorns to do a similar job for West Bromwich Albion and then in 1988 United brought him back to Old Trafford to work with Brian Kidd on the junior coaching staff – he was delighted. Nowadays, Nobby looks less like a sportsman with his thick black-rimmed glasses, but it wasn't too long ago that 'El Bandido', as the Argentinians had named him, struck fear into his opponents.

He won most of the honours available to a footballer – 2 League Championship medals, a European Cup winner's medal, England caps at Youth, Under-23 and full levels and a World Cup Winners' medal.

MANCHESTER EVENING NEWS

MIKE SUMMERBEE

Birthplace: Cheltenham
Born: 15th December 1942
Position: Winger

Football League Career

	Appearances	Goals
Swindon Town	218	39
Manchester City	355 (2)	47
Burnley	51	0
Blackpool	3	0
Stockport County	86 (1)	6
Total	713 (3)	92

England International	Appearances	8
Goals		1

Mike Summerbee was a West Country boy from a footballing family, his uncle George having been a professional with Chester, Preston and Barrow. When Mike left school, he played for his home town club Cheltenham, until Swindon Town spotted his potential. He played more than 200 games for Swindon, helping them clinch promotion from Division Three in 1963. Inevitably, his dashing excursions along the wings caught the eye of some of the bigger clubs and in August 1965, he became the first of Joe Mercer's signings, when Manchester City paid £30,000 to sign him.

He joined City at the time England manager Alf Ramsey was beginning to dispense with wingers on the international scene, but he quickly adapted to the demands being made on the new breed of midfield wide men.

In his first season, he helped City to win the Second Division title and then in a three year spell between 1968 and 1970 - the most successful period in the club's history - he played a significant role in City's triumphs.

Though he wasn't a prolific goalscorer, he did hit a hat-trick as City beat Reading 7-0 at Elm Park in an F.A. Cup Third Round replay after a goalless draw at Maine Road.

Primarily right-footed, he made an immediate impression at Maine Road with his diligence and industry. He tackled back and shouldered his share of the defensive duties - he was a hard, uncompromising player.

In the F.A. Cup Final of 1969, it was Summerbee who went down the right wing avoiding the challenges of Nish and Woollett to cut the ball back from the dead-ball line for Neil Young to strike home the only goal of the game.

Manchester City's attacking power was their strength at the time of the Mercer-Allison partnership and Summerbee's forays on the right were supported by the running of the more orthodox Tony Coleman on the left to give City a compelling urgency that few other First Division teams could match.

He certainly enjoyed the limelight. A confident player on the field, deputising as a central striker when they had injuries, he was a fashionable dresser off it and part-

owner of a boutique with United's George Best. He won eight full England caps, making his debut against Scotland in 1968. He spent ten years with Manchester City before he moved to Turf Moor in June 1975 for a fee of £25,000. His career later took him to Blackpool and then the player-manager's job at Edgeley Park, where his playing career ended after more than 700 League appearances. A good, skilful player, Mike Summerbee was the working man's winger.

FRANK SWIFT

Birthplace:	Blackpool
Born:	26th Dcember 1913
Died:	6th February 1958
Position:	Goalkeeper

Football League Career

	Appearances	Goals
Manchester City	341	0
Total	341	0

England International Appearances	19
Goals	0

Frank Swift set the standards for goalkeepers before and after the Second World War. Joining Manchester City from Fleetwood on 21st October 1932, he made his league debut on Christmas day the following year against Derby County.

Beginning with his first full season in the League side, Frank Swift was ever-present for four consecutive seasons and missed only one game in 1938-39.

In 1934, he was a member of the successful City side that lifted the F.A. Cup when they beat Portsmouth 2-1. At half-time, Pompey led 1-0, with Swift conceding that he might have saved the goal had he been wearing gloves! Fred Tilson hit two second half goals and on the final whistle the 19-year-old Swift turned to collect his cap and gloves and fainted! Afterwards he said, "Fancy a great strapping fellow like me fainting in front of all those people and the King."

Swifty could fool around with the best of them. He often used to make an acrobatic flying dive that would have the crowd roaring even though he knew the ball was going well wide.

In 1935, he made an apearance for The Rest in a trial match against England, but it was to be after the war when he played in a full international. He won 19 caps for England, his first against Northern Ireland in 1946 and played in many wartime internationals as well as gaining First and Second Division Championship medals along with that 1934 F.A. Cup winners' medal.

He had been skipper of Manchester City for a couple of seasons, when against Italy in 1948, he became the first goalkeeper to captain England. He had a magnificent game, one save from Gabetto; the centre-forward was out of this world, leaving the Italian beating the turf with his fists.

Frank Swift had enormous hands, with a finger span of almost a foot; he would catch the ball in one hand and then hold it over the centre-forward's head, just out of reach – he was loved by the crowd. A spectacular goalkeeper, he was daring and sometimes even headed shots away. He was one of the first goalkeepers to elect to throw the ball to a colleague rather than opt for the usual long kick down the field, most used in those days. An excellent shot-stopper, he was a great personality both on and off the field.

Although he retired in Septemeber 1949, his registration was held by City until May 1955.

Frank Swift was tragically killed in the Munich Air Disaster of 1958 when accompanying Manchester United as a newspaper reporter.

MANCHESTER EVENING NEWS

ERNIE TAYLOR

Birthplace:	Sunderland
Born:	2nd September 1925
Died:	9th April 1985
Position:	Inside-Forward

Football League Career

	Appearances	Goals
Newcastle United	107	19
Blackpool	217	53
Manchester United	22	2
Sunderland	68	11
Total	414	85

England International Appearances	1
Goals	0

Ernie Taylor began his footballing career with Newcastle United, joining the St James' Park playing staff from Hylton Colliery Juniors, County Durham in 1942.

During the war, he served in the Royal Navy submarines before going on to play in over 130 first-team games for the Magpies. In October 1951, he signed for Blackpool for £27,000 – it was just six months after helping Newcastle beat Blackpool in the F.A. Cup Final at Wembley.

He was perhaps the unsung hero of Blackpool's win at Wembley in 1953. It wasn't until Taylor started to hit some slide-rule passes to the feet of Matthews that the great man began to make his mark on the match. He went on to play in 217 League games for the Seasiders before he moved to Old Trafford.

To give Manchester United a chance of surviving in football after the Munich disaster, the Football Association waived its rule which 'Cup-ties' a player once he has played in an F.A. Cup Round in any particular season. The rule prevents him from playing for another club in the same competition, so that if he is transferred, he is sidelined until the following season. United's need for players was desperate and the change in rules allowed Jimmy Murphy to sign Ernie Taylor from Blackpool for £8,000.

Taylor made his United debut in the emotional F.A. Cup match against Sheffield Wednesday and played at Wembley that season, when Bolton ended his dream of picking up a third F.A. Cup winners' medal with three different clubs.

Taylor used his vast experience to put his foot on the ball and direct operations. He only played in 30 League and Cup games for the Reds, but his contribution to the aftermath of Munich had been priceless.

He stood only 5ft 4ins, but was surprisingly lethal in front of goal, scoring 85 League goals in his career. He had the facility to split defences wide open with one devastating pass. Before the end of 1958, this skilful and entertaining inside-forward had returned to his home-town club of Sunderland in a £6,000 deal. After playing 68 games, he went into non-League football with Altrincham and then Irish club, Derry City. He retired in February 1962 and two years later emigrated to New Zealand to go coaching with the Christchurch club, New Brighton. He returned to England to work in the Vauxhall car plant at Hooton, Cheshire.

Ernie Taylor, who died in April 1985, won one full cap, as well as 'B' international honours.

MANCHESTER EVENING NEWS

TOMMY TAYLOR

Birthplace:	Smithies, Nr Barnsley
Born:	29th January 1932
Died:	6th February 1958
Position:	Centre-Forward

Football League Career

	Appearances	Goals
Barnsley	44	26
Manchester United	168	112
Total	212	138

England International Appearances	19
Goals	16

Tommy Taylor was making his name with Barnsley, when he wasn't starring for an Army side. He had been at Oakwell since 1947, when he joined them as an amateur from Smithies United, signing professional in July 1949. He was just what United needed, but he was also wanted by several other clubs – Manchester City, Chelsea, Cardiff and West Brom had all made offers. The chase finally ended, when Barnsley chairman Joe Richards said, "The fee for Tommy Taylor is £30,000." Matt Busby felt that big fees sometimes affect players and offered £29,999, which was accepted!

He made his debut for Manchester United against Preston North End in March 1953, socring two goals as the Reds ran out winners 5-2. He ended the season with 7 goals from his 11 matches. At the end of that campaign, he toured South America with an F.A. XI, playing against Argentina, Chile and Uruguay.

During the following season, he scored 23 goals, including two hat-tricks, against Blackpool in November and against Sheffield Wednesday on Christmas Day as the Reds won 5-2.

Tommy Taylor was the ideal centre-forward, strong and sure both in the air and on the ground. He seemed to climb and then hover in space – it was no wonder he won the ball almost every time. He was also brilliant at nodding the ball precisely to a team-mate, whether it was forwards, backwards or sideways. He held the forward line together superbly. When he headed the ball, it went where he wanted it to go and he could shoot as well – inside the box he was devastating.

A week after making his England debut in the abandoned game against Argentina, he scored his first goal for his country. Although he played twice in the 1954 World Cup Finals, he didn't establish himself as an England regular until he replaced Bolton's Nat Lofthouse in 1956.

When United won the League title in 1955-56, Tommy scored 25 League goals from 33 appearances, including four in the 5-2 beating of Cardiff City. In all matches the following season, he scored 34 goals from 44 appearances, including a hat-trick in United's 10-0 win over R.S.C. Anderlecht in a second-leg European Cup tie – the League title going to Old Trafford again. He also picked up an

F.A. Cup runners-up medal and scored United's late goal in the 2-1 defeat by Aston Villa.

He had helped England to qualify for the 1958 World Cup Finals in Sweden, but by the time they came around, he had tragically lost his life in the Munich disaster. In 189 first-team games for United he scored 128 goals. His had been a magnificent career, which saw him score a goal every 125 minutes of his playing days. Taylor also scored 16 goals in his 19 internationals, including two hat-tricks. His early death at Munich dealt an irreparable blow to football in this country. Another of England's great centre-forwards, Nat Lofthouse, commented, "If he hadn't died at Munich, he would have become the greatest centre-forward of all."

MANCHESTER EVENING NEWS

PETER THOMPSON

Birthplace:	Carlisle	
Born:	27th November 1942	
Position:	Winger	

Football League Career

	Appearances	Goals
Preston North End	121	20
Liverpool	318 (4)	41
Bolton Wanderers	111 (6)	2
Total	550 (10)	63

England International Appearances	16
Goals	0

After playing for Carlisle, Cumberland and England as a schoolboy, he joined the Preston North End groundstaff and turned professional in 1959, the year the legendary Tom Finney retired. He made a big impression when he played his initial League game in September 1960 and soon established himself as one of Preston's most consistent performers. Bill Shankly signed him from Preston for £40,000 in August 1963, in the face of opposition from Everton, Wolverhampton Wanderers and Juventus. The day he signed for Liverpool, Shankly told him he'd be the best player in the world; the fastest thing on two legs and become the 'White Pele'.

He had a great debut for Liverpool against Blackburn Rovers at Ewood Park, forcing the Rovers' defenders to twist and turn in their efforts to stay with him. At the end of his first full season, the Reds had won the League Championship and Thompson gave his best display of the season, scoring two goals in the 5-0 trouncing of Arsenal as Liverpool made certain of the title.

There were those who said he should score more goals. When he did score they were often spectacular and match-winners. In the 1964-65 F.A. Cup semi-final against Chelsea, he waltzed past Hinton and Hollins to hit a superb left-footer out of Bonetti's reach.

The accuracy of his crosses played an important part in establishing Roger Hunt as one of the most feared goalscorers of the time. In 1965-66 it was no coincidence that Thompson played in 40 games and that Hunt scored 27 goals.

Making his international debut against Portugal in 1964, he was a regular in the England side for the next two years, though he was a victim of Alf Ramsey's decision to play the 1966 World Cup without wingers. He played in the 2-1 win over Northern Ireland at Wembley in November 1965, but in the next match against Spain, Alan Ball wore the number seven shirt. The last of Thompson's 16 caps came against Scotland in 1970.

Peter Thompson was a fantastic winger; he could take on defenders in tight situations, go past them with ease and had great speed and superb ball control.

He collected two League Championship medals and an

F.A. Cup winners' medal with Liverpool.

After playing 322 League games for Liverpool and finding himself languishing in the Reserves after being plagued by knee trouble, he moved to Bolton on loan in November 1973.

The Anfield crowd loved him and he remains to this day one of the Liverpool folk heroes.

It was Jimmy Armfield who persuaded him to join Bolton on loan when he was considering retirement. He made his debut for the Wanderers against the Second Division leaders Sunderland, in a game played on a Wednesday afternoon, due to the power strike. Bolton won 1-0 and the fans took him to their hearts immediately and in January 1974, he signed for £18,000 – surely one of the bargain buys of all-time. His form at Bolton helped the club through one of its most exciting periods and promotion to Division One.

He retired in April 1978 after a crowd of over 20,000 attended his testimonial at Burnden Park.

He now runs a residential hotel in the Lake District.

MANCHESTER EVENING NEWS

PHIL THOMPSON

Birthplace:	Liverpool
Born:	21st January 1954
Position:	Defender

Football League Career

	Appearances	Goals
Liverpool	337 (3)	7
Sheffield United	36 (1)	0
Total	373 (4)	7

England International Appearances	42
Goals	1

As a youngster, Phil Thompson stood on the Kop to cheer his favourites, so it was a dream come true when he actually signed on at Anfield. Bill Shankly used to say about Thompson: "He tossed up with a sparrow for legs and lost." Thompson's frail-looking frame gave the impression that he wouldn't make a top-class defender because he lacked the necessary physical attributes. This couldn't be further from the truth, for Phil's determination and skill earned him the captaincy of both Liverpool and England.

Originally a midfielder, he made his debut for Liverpool as substitute at Old Trafford in April 1972. The following season he went on to play in enough matches in a variety of positions to qualify for a Championship medal. Bill Shankly however, spotted potential in Thompson in a different role. With regular centre-back Larry Lloyd injured, it was Thompson that Shanks turned to as Emlyn Hughes' partner.

In the 1974 F.A. Cup Final, he completely shackled the Newcastle United and England centre-forward, Malcolm Macdonald, as Liverpool ran out 3-0 winners in one of the most one-sided post-war Finals. Macdonald had threatened to bring the Reds' defence to their knees!

The Thompson-Hughes combination grew in authority at the heart of the Reds' defence. It was a partnership that played a great part in Liverpool's success as the trophies piled up during the second half of the 1970s.

Thompson was a great reader of the game, often playing his way out of trouble in European style, keeping the ball and setting up attacks with superb distribution.

Liverpool often attacked en masse and it was Phil Thompson who was left at the back ready to deal with any possible breakaways – he was probably the most accomplished British defender in a one-to-one situation.

Having said that, it was Phil Thompson who was involved in that televised and much debated League Cup Final replay of 1977-78 against Notts Forest. When John O'Hare broke away, Thompson chased after him and brought him down just outside the area, but despite Liverpool's strong protests, the referee awarded a penalty and John Robertson tucked it away.

When Emlyn Hughes relinquished his place in the

Liverpool side to Alan Hansen, it was Phil Thompson who took over the captaincy. He was a great motivator, inspiring his team-mates to new heights. As captain, he led the Reds to two League Championships and European Cup success over Real Madrid in 1981.

He played 42 times for England, and had a stint as captain.

At Anfield, Graeme Souness became captain, but Thompson played on and won two further Championship medals.

After 466 appearances for Liverpool, his career on Merseyside came to an end in 1985, after being hit by a crop of injuries. He moved to Sheffield United, but wasn't away for long, for eighteen months later in July 1986, he was invited back to Anfield as a member of the coaching staff.

An excellent central defender, his never-say-die spirit epitomised the Liverpool attitude.

MANCHESTER EVENING NEWS

JOHN TOSHACK

Birthplace: Cardiff
Born: 22nd March 1949
Position: Striker

Football League Career

	Appearances	Goals
Cardiff City	159 (3)	75
Liverpool	169 (3)	74
Swansea City	58 (5)	24
Total	386 (11)	173

Wales International Appearances	40
Goals	13

Born in Cardiff, John shared an interest and ability in cricket; not too surprising when one discovers that Ernie Toshack, an Australian Test cricketer who played against England on 9 occasions in the late 1940s, is a distant relative. John Toshack played cricket for the Welsh Schoolboys XI, but football was his first love. He joined Cardiff City as an apprentice, breaking into the first team in 1965-66, scoring 6 goals in 8 games. He played for Cardiff for six years, setting a pattern of a goal every other game.

Signing for Liverpool in November 1970 for a fee of £110,000 he won over the Reds' fans immediately. In the derby game with Everton, he turned things round after Liverpool had gone two goals down. He scored Liverpool's equalising goal, climbing high above Brian Labone to power in a ferocious header and then nodding down an Alec Lindsay cross for full-back Chris Lawler to clinch a 3-2 victory.

In 1974, a proposed £160,000 move to Leicester City was called off because he failed a medical examination.

Toshack's most prolific season was 1975-76 when he scored 23 goals, including three hat-tricks as Liverpool won the League Championship and the U.E.F.A. Cup.

The partnership he established with Kevin Keegan made the pair of them the most feared attacking force in the First Division. They were almost impossible to contain, some of the press claiming that they had some telepathic understanding!

In his seven seasons at Liverpool he scored 95 goals in 236 appearances. It was his heading ability that won him most of his accolades. He gained a reputation for scoring with far post headers, though to be fair, he also possessed a deceptively neat touch on the ground.

For most of his Anfield career he was dogged by a nagging thigh injury and if one looks through the record books, it will come to light that only once did he exceed 30 League games in a season. In March 1978, though there was a host of English and foreign clubs trying to sign him, Liverpool let him go on a free transfer to become player-manager at Swansea. He scored on his debut in a 3-3 draw and went on to score 6 goals in 13 matches, helping

LIVERPOOL DAILY POST & ECHO

Swansea to clinch third place and promotion to Division Three.

In a three year spell with Toshack as their manager, Swansea climbed from the Fourth to the First Division – a feat unrivalled in Football League history.

There have been two occasions when Toshack was being tipped as the new manager at Anfield. The first was when Swansea actually sat at the top of the First Division, the other of course was more recently when Kenny Dalglish resigned.

Toshack won the last of his 40 caps for Wales in 1979 whilst playing for Swansea City. He had made his international debut while at Cardiff, but the bulk of his caps and goals came during his Anfield career.

Sadly, it all went wrong for Toshack, as the Welsh club had debts of more than £1 million from his spending in the transfer market and the team began to disintegrate at an alarming rate. He resigned with 18 months of his contract still to run and asked for no compensation. He returned eight weeks later, but couldn't halt the slide and was sacked. After managing Sporting Lisbon, he bounced back in 1986 as manager at Real Sociedad, winning the Spanish Cup by beating Athletico Madrid in his first season. Later he managed Real Madrid, confirming his place as one of the greatest names in Welsh footballing history.

BERT TRAUTMANN

Birthplace:	Bremen
Born:	22nd October 1923
Position:	Goalkeeper

Football League Career

	Appearances	Goals
Manchester City	508	0
Total	508	0

Arriving in England in April 1945, it was at a Prisoner of War camp at Ashton-in-Makerfield that Bert Trautmann first tried his hand at goalkeeping. He said later that it was his training as a German paratrooper that helped him cushion the ball as he fell. At the end of the Second World War, he was released from the Prisoner of War camp and went to work on a farm and began to play for St Helens Town. After some impressive displays, he signed for City on 2nd November 1949. Seventeen days later, he made his first-team debut for City against Bolton Wanderers.

Of course, replacing the great and very popular Frank Swift, Trautmann came in for a great deal of hostility from the Maine Road supporters. This perhaps was not surprising, for the war was still fresh in the minds of many people and as an ex-German paratrooper and Prisoner of War, he could hardly have expected the warmest of Lancashire welcomes.

Later marrying the City club secretary's daughter, he soon won over the hearts of the Maine Road followers.

Trautmann was a member of the victorious City side of 1956 that lifted the F.A. Cup, beating Birmingham City 3-1 at Wembley. With just fifteen minutes remaining, Bert Trautmann dived to save at the feet of Peter Murphy, the Birmingham inside-forward, and was caught in the neck by his knee. After receiving lengthy treatment, the goalkeeper continued courageously, though he was obviously in great pain. It was only after the match had finished that it was discovered that he had played the closing minutes with a broken neck. He missed the chance to play for his native Germany, being out of the game for the next seven months.

There is no doubt though, if he'd been born in this country, he would have gone on to play for England.

Besides his two appearances for City in F.A. Cup Finals at Wembley, he was voted the 1956 Footballer of the Year. He also had to overcome personal tragedy that same year, when his five-year-old son was killed in a road accident. He retired on 10th May 1964, after playing in over 500 games for City. His testimonial match on Maine Road saw a combined City/United eleven face an international eleven before nearly 48,000 fans. The game had barely warmed up when United's Maurice Setters, in unfamiliar sky blue, killed the ball, turned, and with immense power fired a shot past Trautmann and danced for joy at his own goal. "I've always wanted to score against Bert", he said later, "and tonight was going to be my last chance. I couldn't resist it."

He later played for non-League Wellington Town and then became general manager of Stockport County, before going to coach abroad.

Still a frequent visitor to these shores, it was only earlier this year that he came to Burnden Park to meet his old friend and opponent, NatLofthouse.

MANCHESTER EVENING NEWS

ROY VERNON

Birthplace: Prestatyn
Born: 14th April 1937
Position: Inside-Forward

Football League Career

	Appearances	Goals
Blackburn Rovers	131	49
Everton	176	101
Stoke City	84 (3)	22
Halifax Town	4	0
Total	395 (3)	172

Wales International Appearances	32
Goals	8

When Roy Vernon left school in Prestatyn, he declined the offer to go to Everton, but joined the Blackburn Rovers ground-staff. There he developed under the watchful eye of the then Blackburn manager, Johnny Carey.

He made his League debut for the Rovers in September 1955 at the age of 18. Within twelve months, Vernon was a regular member of the Blackburn first-team, displaying a maturity far beyond his years.

He was a creative player who struck a dead ball with tremendous power. Dark, lean and lithe, he had great acceleration and was the deadliest of finishers. Vernon graduated to the Welsh squad in time to be involved in the 1958 World Cup Final Tournament. His best season for Blackburn was 1958-59, when he scored 17 goals in his 38 appearances.

When Johnny Carey left to manage Everton, Vernon began to clash with the new Rovers manager, Dally Duncan. Meanwhile, at Goodison, the search was on to find a centre-forward who could link up with the diminutive Scot, Bobby Collins. There were a number around, but they were of course expensive, but with Blues Chairman John Moores encouraging the club to be more expensive, the possibilities opened up. Top of the list was Roy Vernon. So in February 1960, he followed his mentor to Goodison Park in a £27,000 deal which brought Eddie Thomas to Blackburn in part-exchange.

In his first full season, he was magnificent, knocking in 21 goals with Collins scoring 16. He was top scorer again the following season, after Collins' departure to Leeds, with 26 goals, striking up a good understanding with the newly arrived Alex Young.

Vernon was the architect of Everton's Championship victory of 1962-63. As the last game of the season approached, Everton needed to beat Fulham at home to clinch the title. He hit a magnificent hat-trick in a 4-1 win and finished the season with 24 League goals.

He top-scored again in 1963-64 with 18 goals from 31 matches; by now he had developed into one of the finest creative players in the early 1960s and was the Everton captain.

The arrival of Fred Pickering at Goodison heralded the departure of Roy Vernon in March 1956 to Stoke City for £40,000. He had performed the role of striker very well, scoring 110 goals in just under 200 games for the Blues. He had won 32 Welsh caps, the last of these being against Scotland in 1963. He was as dangerous as any striker in the First Division at that time and had been a fine servant to the club during his six seasons.

In January 1970, he had a brief loan spell with Halifax Town and then spent some time playing in South Africa. Eight months later, this talented inside-forward of all-round ability, returned to the north-west to team up with former Blackburn colleagues, Ronnie Clayton and Bryan Douglas, playing at Great Harwood.

MANCHESTER EVENING NEWS

DENNIS VIOLLET

Birthplace:	Manchester
Born:	20th September 1933
Position:	Forward

Football League Career

	Appearances	Goals
Manchester United	259	160
Stoke City	181 (1)	59
Total	440 (1)	219

England International Appearances	2
Goals	1

Dennis Viollet was an England Schoolboy international and turned professional with United in September 1950 after just two years in the Reds' junior ranks. There could well have been a snag to Denis becoming a United player ... he lived near Maine Road and his parents were supporters of Manchester City. Yet after Matt Busby, Jimmy Murphy and Bert Whalley had chatted with the family, both parents seemed happy for Dennis to wear the red of United.

He made his League debut for the Reds in a 2-1 win at St James' Park, Newcastle, in April 1953, succeeding Stan Pearson.

Frail in appearance, his skills and stamina belied his frame. Viollet was a player who snapped up the half-chances at a terrific rate. In his 13 years with United, he scored seven hat-tricks; the first coming in October 1954, as the Reds won a remarkable match at Stamford Bridge, beating Chelsea 6-5. He then proceeded to score a hat-trick in each of the next six seasons, though he was on the losing side at Turf Moor in October 1960 when United lost 3-5.

He won League Championship medals with United in 1955-56 and 1956-57 and an F.A. Cup runners-up medal. In 1959-60, he scored 32 League goals - it is still a United record. In all matches for United, he scored 178 goals, 160 of them coming in his 259 League games. Viollet was a compelling performer at inside or centre-forward, possessing superb ball control, a delicate body-swerve and with a powerful shot. He played in 12 European ties for the Reds and scored 13 goals.

Viollet moved to Stoke City in a £25,000 deal in January 1962. In his five and a half years at the Victoria Ground, he added 59 League goals in 182 appearances, helping the Potters to the Second Division Championship in 1962-63. He then spent 18 months in the United States, playing in the N.A.S.L. with Baltimore Bays. He returned to these shores to play for non-League Witton Albion, but six months later, he joined Linfield as their player-manager and won an Irish F.A. Cup winners' medal. He later coached at Preston and then Crewe, managing the Gresty Road outfit for six months in 1971.

In 1976-77, he returned to the States to coach N.A.S.L.

team, Washington Diplomats.

He represented the Football League in the late fifties and was capped twice by the full England team in 1960 and 1961.

MANCHESTER EVENING NEWS

CHARLIE WAYMAN

Birthplace:	Bishop Auckland
Born:	16th May 1922
Position:	Forward

Football League Career

	Appearances	Goals
Newcastle United	47	32
Southampton	100	73
Preston North End	157	104
Middlesbrough	55	31
Darlington	23	14
Total	382	254

Starting his career with Newcastle United, the Bishop Auckland born forward topped the Second Division goalscoring charts in 1946-47 with 30 goals. Transferred to Southampton, he once again topped the Division Two charts with 32 goals.

It was one of his performances for the Saints that season against North End, that led to his transfer to the Deepdale club. Harry Makinson, the Preston centre-half, was marking Wayman that day, as this diamond from the north-east's bottomless mine of talent took the major honours by scoring a hat-trick in Southampton's 3-0 home win.

It was Preston manager Will Scott who visualised the neat and skilful Wayman as a perfect foil to both Finney and Beattie. He joined North End in September 1950, in part-exchange for the dashing Eddie Brown. He had a big share in North End's 1950-51 record-breaking romp to promotion as they piled up feats like 10 away wins, 20 games without defeat and 14 successive League wins.

Charlie Wayman soon proved his worth and never more so than when he scored four first-half goals against Queen's Park Rangers in London one Christmas Day. His flair for snatching scintillating goals also earned him a memorable hat-trick at Highbury against Arsenal.

His delectable artistry made his four years at Deepdale nostalgic reminders of happy days.

His totals in four seasons were 27, 25, 24 (topping the Division One goalscoring charts) and 25.

He scored when Preston lost the 1954 F.A. Cup Final – Wayman's contribution to the Wembley run was six goals in eight games. A genuine match-winner, he scored 12 in his 14 cup-ties.

Wayman was a tremendous poacher of goals, always being in the right place at the right time.

He added another six goals in six games at the beginning of the 1954-55 season, when manager Frank Hill created a local outcry by transferring him to Middlesbrough.

Charlie's average goal yield for North End was two for every three appearances.

Maybe he had begun to lose a little of his nip, but Preston had to drop all the five players subsequently tried in his position that season.

After 55 League games with Middlesbrough, he joined Darlington, before becoming coach at Northern League club Evenwood Town. Wayman was one of a select band of players to score over 250 League goals in his career. Father of six, Charlie Wayman was a little giant with a big heart, who never forgot to bring his children presents after North End trips to the capital.

WALLY & HOWARD TALBOT PHOTOGRAPHY

NORMAN WHITESIDE

Birthplace:	Belfast
Born:	8th May 1965
Position:	Forward; Midfield

Football League Career

	Appearances	Goals	
Manchester United	193 (13)	47	
Everton	29 (2)	9	
Total	222 (15)		56

Northern Ireland International Appearances	38
Goals	9

Norman Whiteside has always been ahead of his time in terms of both skill and physical development. It was the Boys' Brigade that gave Whiteside his first real taste of representative football. He scored a century of goals in one season, before he was discovered by United's Belfast scout, Bob Bishop. After being signed by United at the age of 15, he made his League debut as a substitute a year later in a 1-0 win over Brighton. On his full debut, he grabbed the fans' attention by scoring in a 2-0 win over Stoke City – he was 17 years 8 days old.

Even as a boy, he had been tall and strongly built and had confidence in his passing, shooting, running and tackling. These inevitably earned him comparisons with the great George Best, but Whiteside has admitted that he modelled himself on the now Hearts manager, Joe Jordan.

Norman Whiteside stepped out to make his World Cup debut in 1982 with all the confidence of a player who has done it all, yet he was just 17 years and 41 days old when he pulled on the emerald green shirt of Northern Ireland against Yugoslavia in Zaragosa. He was the youngest player ever to appear in a World Cup finals tournament. He wasn't only the youngest to appear in a World Cup finals match, he was also the youngest to be booked, being shown the yellow card in his first match!

In 1983, Italian giants A.C. Milan offered Manchester United £1.5 million for Whiteside. Rather surprisingly, manager Ron Atkinson and Chairman Martin Edwards agreed to the deal, but Norman wanted to continue his career at Old Trafford. It was also a year that he demonstrated his keen goalscoring ability, scoring against Liverpool in the League Cup Final and again in United's 4-0 replay win over Brighton in the F.A. Cup Final. After that season, he became even more of a key member of the Old Trafford set-up, using his strength and power and captaining the side when Robson was injured.

Against Everton in the 1985 F.A. Cup Final, he scored a majestic winner, worthy to win any Cup Final. It was a booming left foot shot, so superbly swung and placed, it cut between two defenders and entered the net just beyond Southall's dive.

When Whiteside was a teenager, Northern Ireland manager Billy Bingham was often heard to remark, "19

LIVERPOOL DAILY POST & ECHO

going on 30" - confirming a maturity beyond his years. When he went to the 1986 World Cup Finals in Mexico, he became the yougest player ever to appear in two World Cup tournaments. Although Northern Ireland were eliminated, he scored in their 1-0 win over Algeria, where he was by far the most effective player on the pitch.

His lack of pace has often gone against him, but his ability to hold the ball and sheer power makes him the most uncomfortable of opponents. Sadly, a serious achilles tendon injury which threatened his career, and a clash of personalities with manager Alex Ferguson, soured his last days at United.

In July 1989, he was transferred to Everton for £650,000 and at just 24 years of age, he was hoping to put some of the sparkle back into his game. Within two months, he had been recalled to the Northern Ireland side as captain and scored in a World Cup qualifier against Hungary.

RAY WILSON

Birthplace: Shirebrook
Born: 17th December 1934
Position: Full-Back

Football League Career

	Appearances	Goals
Huddersfield Town	266	6
Everton	114 (2)	0
Oldham Athletic	25	0
Bradford City	2	0
Total	407 (2)	6

England International Appearances	63
Goals	0

Born in the Derbyshire pit village of Shirebrook, Ray Wilson had no burning ambition to be a professional footballer, but did play for his local youth club. One day, the youth club had no game and Ray was asked to turn out for an open age side and scored all his sides' goals in a 6-3 defeat. He was asked to go for a trial with Huddersfield Town and they immediately offered him terms as an apprentice professional. At Leeds Road, he came under the expert eye of coach Ray Goodall, who with Sam Wadsworth had formed the legendary full-back partnership of the Huddersfield side that won the League Championship in three successive seasons between 1924 and 1926.

When he returned from National Service in 1955, he was still playing at inside-left; it was Goodall who switched him with great success to full-back.

He made his League debut for Huddersfield in October 1955 against Manchester United in a First Division match. He played in six games that season, but Town still went down.

Ray Wilson arrived at Goodison in June 1964 in a £50,000 deal that took Mick Meagan in the opposite direction. He was now 29 and already had 266 League games under his belt in a nine year career with Second Division Huddersfield. He had already played 30 times for England and was regarded as the best left-back in Europe.

He helped Everton win the F.A. Cup in 1966 and then played his part in England's magnificent World Cup triumph. He was the only Everton player in Alf Ramsey's victorious side, for Alan Ball was still with Blackpool at that time.

He went on to play for Everton in the 1968 F.A. Cup Final as Everton lost to West Bromwich Albion, Jeff Astle scoring the only goal of the game.

A competent defender, he was composed and looked in command even in the most difficult of situations. He always played to his strengths and if he did have a weakness, it was his heading. Ray will never forget his headed clearance that gifted Haller the opening goal of the 1966 World Cup Final. From that moment on though, he never put a foot wrong. He won 63 caps for England, which was a record for a full-back for almost twenty years until it was surpassed by Kenny Sansom.

On May 16th 1969, Ray Wilson was given a free transfer. He had twisted his knee prior to the start of the 1968-69 campaign and though he tried to come back as the season progressed, it never felt right and he had to call it a day at Goodison.

He was a great influence in the four years he was at Everton. I'm sure if he'd joined the club ten years earlier than he did, he would have been one of the all-time greats.

In 1969 at the age of 35 he joined Oldham Athletic for a season and a year later went to Bradford City as player-coach. He played in over 400 games in an injury-stricken career of fifteen years.

One of the finest left-backs in footballing history, he built up a successful career as an undertaker when he finally retired from the game.

LIVERPOOL DAILY POST & ECHO

FRANK WORTHINGTON

Birthplace: Halifax
Born: 23rd November 1948
Position: Forward

Football League Career

	Appearances	Goals
Huddersfield Town	166 (5)	42
Leicester City	209 (1)	72
Bolton Wanderers	81 (3)	35
Birmingham City	71(4)	30
Leeds United	32	14
Sunderland	18 (1)	2
Southampton	34	4
Brighton Hove Albion	27 (4)	7
Tranmere Rovers	51 (8)	21
Preston North End	10 (13)	3
Stockport County	18 (1)	6
Total	717 (40)	236

England International Appearances 8
Goals 2

From a footballing family – older brothers Bob and Dave, both full-backs, had long League careers – Frank started his career with Huddersfield Town in 1963 and turned professional in November 1966. He made 171 League appearances for Huddersfield, helping them win the Second Division title in 1970.

At the end of the 1971-72 season, Huddersfield finished bottom of the First Division and the chance came for him to join Liverpool. A fee of £150,000 had been agreed and Worthington duly arrived at Anfield to sign. He was a Liverpool player, subject to a medical examination. The club doctor revealed that Frank had high blood pressure – he had failed the medical.

Leicester City seized their chance and a cut-price Worthington moved on for £80,000. In 1974, Frank's elegantly effective centre-forward play was rewarded with an England call-up from Sir Alf Ramsey. He held his place under caretaker manager Joe Mercer and went on to make eight appearances. Frank was at that time an international class player and should have made many more appearances for his country.

His old Huddersfield boss Ian Greaves was searching for that extra quality to lift Bolton Wanderers into the First Division after two agonising near-misses. He came to Bolton on loan in September 1977 and scored on his debut against Stoke City. He was signed permanently for £90,000 and soon rediscovered the style which had made him one of the best strikers in the game – the ice-cool finishing, the keen positional sense, the close control in tight spots and the neat headed flick-ons.

Frank and his co-striker Neil Whatmore banged in 30 goals between them as Wanderers took the Second Division title. It was his goal at Blackburn that finally clinched the promotion.

The following season, Frank proved his class both as a target man and a finisher. Although Bolton struggled against relegation for a while, Frank ended the season with 24 League goals to top the First Division goalscoring charts. Bolton did the double over Manchester United that season, winning 3-0 at Burnden and 2-1 at Old Trafford, with Frank hitting two goals in each match; the second in injury time at Old Trafford took him past his career-best total for a season. His televised goal against Ipswich Town that season won the Goal of the Season competition.

In October 1980, after a summer in the North America Soccer League with Philadelphia Furies, the player who had become a hero at Bolton in what was a relatively short career there, was sold to Birmingham City for £150,000. He top-scored there and helped them win promotion before moves to Leeds United (£100,000) and Sunderland (£50,000). The First Division welcomed him back with Southampton, before spells with Brighton, Tranmere (as player-manager), Preston and Stockport County.

One of the game's most gifted and colourful strikers, he made 757 League appearances in a career that saw him approaching his fortieth birthday before he left the first-class game.

MANCHESTER EVENING NEWS

RON YEATS

Birthplace: Aberdeen
Born: 15th November 1937
Position: Centre-Half

Football League Career

	Appearances	Goals
Liverpool	357 (1)	13
Tranmere Rovers	97	5
Total	454 (1)	18

Scotland International Appearances	2
Goals	0

Bill Shankly's admiration for the 6ft 2ins Scot dated back to when he was manager of Huddersfield Town. He had attempted to sign him from Dundee United then, but the Leeds Road club could not afford the asking price. When installed at Anfield, Shanks failed in an attempt to bring Jack Charlton from Leeds, so went to Tannadice and paid £30,000 for the man he knew would be the backbone of his first great side.

Shanks called him 'a colossus in defence' – the description was an apt one. Within five months of his arrival in the summer of 1961, he had been made skipper. In his first season, the Reds galloped to promotion, not many centre-forwards finding a way past him!

In the First Division, Ron Yeats proved to be the most dominant in the air, whilst on the ground his tremendous tackling and sensible distribution went to prove what a great capture he had been.

He was an inspiring captain, leading the Reds to two Championships and a succession of superb European matches.

The 1965 F.A. Cup campaign saw Yeats produce some of his most outstanding performances. In the third round at the Hawthorns, he picked up the ball in his own penalty area when somebody in the crowd blew a whistle. Justice was done, when Albion's Bobby Cram blasted the ball high and wide. In the fifth round at Burnden Park, he pulled a muscle after only nine minutes, but still went on to keep Wanderers' Wyn Davies in check. In the sixth round, he laid on the winner for Roger Hunt and then completely dominated Leeds United and England centre-forward Alan Peacock in the final.

Throughout the sixties, Yeats was still essentially a rugged centre-half, but as the decade wore on, he grew more accomplished. Off the field, he was a great influence on the younger players on the Anfield staff and though quietly spoken, his imposing personality made him the ideal choice for dealing with the Liverpool management. After losing his place to Larry Lloyd, he still contributed a valuable spell at left-back. Nicknamed 'Rowdy' after Clint Eastwood's TV cowboy of that era, he made the short trip to Prenton Park, where he made 97 League appearances for the Birkenhead club. He later managed

Tranmere Rovers before ending his managerial career with Barrow. A player who will go down in Liverpool folklore, he is at present the Anfield club's chief scout.

LIVERPOOL DAILY POST & ECHO

ALEX YOUNG

Birthplace:	Loanhead
Born:	3rd February 1937
Position:	Forward

Football League Career

	Appearances	Goals
Everton	227 (1)	77
Stockport County	23	5
Total	250 (1)	82

Scotland International Appearances	8
Goals	5

Born in Loanhead, Alex Young signed for Scottish club Heart of Midlothian from Newtongrange Star as an 18-year-old. In five seasons with the Tynecastle club, he scored 77 goals, including 20 in the club's record-breaking 1957-58 Championship campaign and 23 when they recaptured the title in 1959-60.

Signed from Hearts on 23rd November 1960 in a £55,000 deal that brought team-mate and full-back George Thomson to Goodison, Alex Young soon won over the Everton fans with his class.

He didn't make his Everton debut until 17th December against Tottenham Hotspur because he arrived on Merseyside carrying a nasty knee injury sustained in playing for the British Army. It wasn't the best of results, Everton losing 3-1. From then on that season, Young and Roy Vernon began to blossom as a partnership and after he hit his first goals for the club, a double against Blackburn Rovers, there was no holding them. Everton won six out of the last seven games of the season to finish fifth in the First Division.

In the Championship winning season of 1962-63, he scored in each of the opening three games, all victories. He ended the season with 22 goals, including the only goal of the game against Tottenham Hotspur that took Everton to the top of the League – a position they were never dislodged from.

He was arguably the greatest Scottish player to sign for Everton and was a major influence on the Everton side that beat Sheffield Wednesday 3-2 in the 1966 F.A. Cup Final.

In attacking situations, he always seemed to have plenty of time. He knew where to play the ball instinctively – he didn't have to look where he was passing; he was aware of all the options open to him without looking up. For all his flair and grace, he possessed a vicious shot and had good heading ability.

Yet for all his subtlety, skill and natural ability, he only played for Scotland on 8 occasions, making his debut in 1960 in a 1-1 draw with England – he surely should have played many more times. Like many players with flair and genius, he set himself very high standards and was often very critical of his own game.

His blond hair made him quite a distinctive figure on the field and the fans called him the 'Golden Vision'. He was a gifted, elegant striker and when he was replaced near the end of his career, there was a public outcry! He was replaced by a 16-year-old youngster by the name of Joe Royle for a game at Blackpool. Manager Harry Catterick was assaulted by outraged Everton supporters – such was Young's popularity.

In August 1968 at the age of only 31, Alex Young became player-manager of Glentoran. He only spent two months across the sea before returning to join Stockport County. After only 23 games for the men from Edgeley Park he was forced to retire with knee trouble in August 1969.

Alex Young was without doubt one of the classiest players in post-war football. His fans worshipped him; to them he was the Greatest!

MANCHESTER EVENING NEWS

Other titles published in paperback by Didsbury Press

Farewell Manchester: the Story of the 1939 Evacuation, by Audrey Jones

Outrages, Fatal and Other: A Chronicle of Cheshire Crime 1612-1912, by Derek Yarwood

Mediterraneans — A review of new writing from, or about the Mediterranean region, edited by Kenneth Brown and Robert Waterhouse. Available on subscription.

Growing up in Manchester, by Bill Griffiths

Lancashire Miscellany, by Dean Hayes

Ask your bookshop to contact the publisher for copies on 061 434 6495. In case of difficulty, contact the publisher for advice.

... and anyway, we would like you to tell us if any of your favourite Lancashire Greats are not included in this book, and why you think they deserve inclusion. We promise to pass all your written comments on to the author, Dean Hayes. So write to Didsbury Press at 7 Darley Avenue, Didsbury, Manchester, M20 8XE or send a fax to 061 445 8155.